NIGELLA BITES

Also by Nigella Lawson

HOW TO EAT
THE PLEASURES AND PRINCIPLES OF GOOD FOOD

HOW TO BE A DOMESTIC GODDESS
BAKING AND THE ART OF COMFORT COOKING

NIGELLA BITES

NIGELLA LAWSON
PHOTOGRAPHS BY FRANCESCA YORKE

Chatto & Windus
LONDON

First published in 2001

3 5 7 9 8 6 4

First published in the United Kingdom in 2001 by Chatto & Windus
Random House, 20 Vauxhall Bridge Road, London SW1V 2SA

Random House Australia (Pty) Limited
20 Alfred Street, Milsons Point, Sydney, New South Wales 2061, Australia

Random House New Zealand Limited
18 Poland Road, Glenfield, Auckland 10, New Zealand

Random House South Africa (Pty) Limited
Endulini, 5a Jubilee Road, Parktown 2193, South Africa

The Random House Group Limited Reg. No. 954009

www.randomhouse.co.uk

A CIP catalogue record for this book is available from the British Library.

ISBN 0 7011 7287 8

Design and Art Direction: Caz Hildebrand
Cookery Assistant: Hettie Potter
Stylist: Helen Trent

Papers used by The Random House Group Limited are natural, recyclable products made from wood grown in sustainable forests. The manufacturing processes conform to the environmental regulations of the country of origin.

Printed by Appl Druck, Wemding, Germany

CONTENTS

PREFACE

To tell the truth, I didn't intend to write another book so soon. Not that this is by way of an apology: I am too evangelical about the food I like eating (and cooking) not to want to present the recipes from the new series of *Nigella Bites* to you, taking advantage of the extra wittering space a book allows. But I've wanted, too, to borrow from the other medium, so this book is slightly different from my previous two: there are more pictures and the chapters inevitably take their shape and content from each programme in the TV series.

In truth, there isn't a conflict. I've always felt that food is nothing if taken out of the context in which it's eaten, and the programmes – and consequently these chapters – are arranged according to the sort of cooking we might want to do, depending on our life, our timetable and our mood. But, please: these are suggestions only, not inflexible command. Life is not so rigidly constructed, and I might well want to cook something for a weekday dinner that I've earmarked here for a Sunday lunch, and presume you might, too.

Anyway, even if themes, the focus of these chapters, are varied, what remains constant, and so what links them, is taste. I don't mean taste in a food-snobbish, status sense (please, I am just not interested) but the tendency towards certain techniques (for me, that means easy ones) and certain ingredients. Restaurant chefs rely, to a greater or lesser extent, on innovation and novelty; what's more, they are generally less constrained by ordinary domestic concerns of budget or storage space. They can buy a bottle of some special liqueur for one particular recipe; we are unlikely to. So, you might well find that certain ingredients crop up repeatedly. In the same way, when a little bit of stock is needed, I'm not going to instruct you to start boiling up bones left, right and centre, just for the purist sake of it, but rather suggest you use the shop-bought stock-concentrate I use myself. The point is, this is the way we cook at home. And for all that this is, frankly, the book of the television series, I am neither a chef nor a performer: none of the recipes here has been specially constructed for broadcast or publication purposes: this is the food

I cook, the food I eat.

At the end of each chapter, I've left a page or two for notes. I wanted to do this for a variety of reasons. It's hardly, in fact, a novel practice: the idea first came to me after riffling through the old, battered books belonging to my grandmothers and my friends' mothers; I found I learnt as much from reading their scribbled comments and amendments; it's what made the food come alive for me. Besides, it seemed to me that a book linked to a television series might be used, be read, in a particular way. True, there is slightly more in the book than in the series (where recipes had to be lost because of constraints of broadcast time I've resisted dropping them from the published version), but it seemed to me that while watching the programmes, some of you might want to jot things down in the book that accompanies them.

But most of all, this idea came to me out of the various book signings I've done. Occasionally, people apologise for not coming and buying a new book but rather bringing their own, already stained and dog-eared copies. Believe me, there's no need to apologise: I can't tell you how much this means to me. And the sort of cookery book that's splattered and scribbled over is the only sort of cookery book I want to write. I'm not interested in barking instructions: this isn't meant to be a monologue. As I've said before, I want to be there in the kitchen with you; my words are merely my side of the conversation I imagine we might have. The pages for notes, then, are there for you to make your own response.

CONVERSION CHARTS

OVEN TEMPERATURES

gas mark	°C		description
1	140		very cool
2	150		cool
3	160		warm
4	180		moderate
5	190	}	fairly hot
6	200		
7	210		hot
8	220	}	very hot
9	240		

Weights		Volumes	
ounces	grams	fluid ounces	millilitres
1	25	1	25
2	50	2	55
3	75	3	75
4	110	4	120
5	150	5	150
6	175	6	175
7	200	7	200
8	225	8	225
9	250	9	250
10	275	10	275
11	315	15	425
12	350	20/1 pint	570
13	365	$1^{1}/_{4}$ pints	725
14	400	$1^{1}/_{2}$ pints	850
15	425	$1^{3}/_{4}$ pints	1 litre
16/1lb	450		

NOTE: Eggs, where specified, are large (and preferably organic and free-range); all butter is unsalted, and salmon and meat organic, for preference.

CHAPTER ONE

ALL-DAY BREAKFAST

While breakfast in the table-laden, leisurely sense might not be an option in our everyday lives, weekends make something a bit more greedy and ceremonial possible. Or just refuse to be constrained by the orthodox timetable and make late-lie-in breakfast food for whatever time of day you want.

ORANGE BREAKFAST MUFFINS

If you're going to attempt anything other than a bowl of cereal for an ordinary weekday breakfast, then muffins are the best bet. They are the easiest things to make, not least because the laziest of stirring is what's required. The truth is that a heavy, lumpy batter makes for the lightest muffin. Having said that – and this holds true for the recipe below, too, of course – no homemade muffin is ever going to be as risen and aeratedly humped as a factory-produced one, and nor should it be. The point is a muffin is not a cake. I presume anyway that they were originally devised to be eaten in much the same way as the yeasted version, that's to say as a form of sweet, tender roll with jam. And that's exactly how I eat these. Split them still warm and, mouthful by mouthful, smear with the best unsalted butter you can find, adding as you want, marmalade, jam or amber, liquid-light honey.

75g unsalted butter
250g self-raising flour
25g ground almonds
½ teaspoon bicarbonate of soda
1 teaspoon baking powder
75g caster sugar

zest of 1 orange
100ml freshly squeezed orange juice
100ml full-fat milk
1 egg
12-bun muffin tray lined with 12 paper cases

Preheat the oven to 200°C/gas mark 6.

Melt the butter and set aside. Combine the flour, ground almonds, bicarb, baking powder, sugar and orange zest in a large bowl. Measure the orange juice and milk into a jug and whisk in the egg and then the cooled, melted butter. Now pour the liquid ingredients into the dry ingredients, mixing with a fork as you go. The batter will be lumpy but that's as it should be: you want everything to be no more than barely combined. The whole point of muffin mixture is that it must never be overworked.

Spoon out the mixture equally into the muffin cases and cook for 20 minutes. Remove, in their paper cases, to a wire rack and let cool slightly (but not completely) before devouring.

Makes 12.

WELSH-RAREBIT MUFFINS

I got the idea for these from one of my Amazon-trawled titles, one of those ring-bound American books, called magnificently (and appropriately) *The Joy of Muffins* (by Genevieve Farrow and Diane Dreher). This is my version, and is great by itself or with a plate of burnt and sticky-skinned sausages.

for the muffins:
225g self-raising flour
50g rye flour
1 teaspoon baking powder
½ teaspoon bicarbonate of soda
1 teaspoon salt
1 teaspoon English mustard powder
125g strong Cheddar, grated
6 tablespoons vegetable oil

150g Greek yoghurt
125ml full-fat milk
1 egg
2 tablespoons Worcestershire sauce
12-bun muffin tray lined with 12 cases

for the topping:
25g strong Cheddar, grated
more Worcestershire sauce for sprinkling

Preheat oven to 200°C/gas mark 6.

Mix the flours, baking powder, bicarb, salt, mustard powder and cheese in a large bowl with a fork. In a large measuring jug, beat together the remaining ingredients. Pour into the dry ingredients, mixing lightly with your fork, remembering that good muffins are made from lumpy batter.

Pour into the muffin tins and cook for 20 minutes, then quickly take them out of the oven and put a little cheese and a sprinkling of Worcestershire sauce on each one. Put them back in the oven for another 5 minutes, then put the muffins on a baking tray to cool. Eat them while they are still warm but not hot.

Makes 12.

AMERICAN PANCAKES WITH WAFER-BACON AND MAPLE SYRUP

While American pancakes with syrup are undeniably a supermom-with-kids breakfast cliché, they are also undeniably good, and in my book – which this is, after all – that alone argues forcefully for their inclusion here. They are anyway very easy to make, easier than thinner English pancakes or crêpes, and it's not hard to get into the weekend habit of mixing them up. They're what I make for my children's breakfast at weekends. I make up half-quantities of the batter (or the full amount on Saturday, saving half of it in a clingfilm-covered jug for Sunday) and let them squeeze golden syrup, rather than the smokier maple, over them; we dispense with the bacon altogether.

Talking of which, if you can, buy pancetta from a deli or a butcher and ask them to slice it finely. This makes for crisp salty wafers, perfect with the resiny sweetness of the syrup. Otherwise ordinary bacon is, of course, fine, though I'd go for streaky rather than back. It's the fat in the bacon that makes it crisp up.

For speed, it makes sense to cook the pancakes in small, dolloped-on rounds, on the griddle or in a non-stick frying pan, but I often use a blini pan, which produces perfect (or as perfect as I am ever going to achieve) 7cm rounds, as in the picture here. The only drawback is that, unless you dot your hob with blini pans – hardly practical or conducive to early morning cheer – this means cooking them one by one.

30g (2 tablespoons) unsalted butter
225g plain flour
2 heaped teaspoons baking powder
1 teaspoon sugar
pinch of salt
300ml full-fat milk
2 eggs

10 rashers streaky bacon or approx.
100g wafer-thin-cut pancetta
1–2 teaspoons vegetable oil for frying bacon
butter for frying pancakes
best-quality maple syrup

Melt the butter and set aside to cool slightly while you get on with the rest of the batter and the bacon.

In a wide-necked jug, measure out the flour and add the baking powder, sugar and salt. Stir to combine.

In another jug, measure out the milk, beat in the eggs and then the slightly cooled butter, and pour this jug of liquid ingredients into the jug of dry ingredients, whisking as you do so. Or just put everything in a blender and blitz.

In the vegetable oil, fry the bacon (cut into half crosswise) or the pancetta strips until crisp, remove to kitchen towels and cover with more kitchen towels (not because I'm fat-phobic – as if! – but because this will help them keep their requisite crispness). Now, heat either a griddle or non-stick frying pan, smear with a small bit of butter and then start frying. I just pour small amounts straight from the jug (but you could use an American quarter-cup measure if you prefer) so that you have wiggly circumferenced discs of about 4cm in diameter. When you see bubbles erupting on the surface, turn the pancakes over and cook for a couple of minutes, if that, on the other side.

Or just use a blini pan and, as above, turn when the bubbles break through to the uncooked surface. There is a Russian saying to the effect that the first pancake is always botched, so be prepared to sacrifice the initial offering to unceremonious stove-side gobbling.

Pile the pancakes onto plates, wigwam with pieces of crispy bacon or pancetta and dribble or pour over, depending on greed and capacity, that clear, brown, woodily fragrant syrup.

Makes about 15 pancakes if cooked in a blini pan; or if not, about 25 pancakes the size of jam-jar lids.

ASIAN-SPICED KEDGEREE

Kedgeree started life, in India, as a dish of lentils and rice and then, translated into the kitchens of what could be called the Anglo-Indian Ascendancy, became an eggy, golden pile of rice punctuated with slabby chunks of smoked haddock. When I was a child it remained as a comforting brunch dish, still part of the homely repertoire of the normal British cook. Here, I've fiddled with it some more, replacing the earthier Indian flavours with the sharper ones of Thailand and South-east Asia and trading the strident tones of the smoked haddock for gentle, fleshy salmon, beautifully coral against the turmeric-stained gold of the rice.

500ml cold water for poaching the fish
2 lime leaves, torn into pieces
4 salmon fillets (approx. 3cm thick), preferably organic, skinned (about 750g in total)
45g unsalted butter
1 teaspoon oil
1 onion, chopped finely
1/2 teaspoon ground coriander

1/2 teaspoon ground cumin
1/2 teaspoon turmeric
225g basmati rice
3 hard-boiled eggs, quartered
3 tablespoons chopped coriander, plus more for sprinkling
juice and zest of a lime plus more lime segments to serve
fish sauce (nam pla) to taste

Preheat the oven to 220°C/gas mark 7. This is because the easiest way to poach the salmon for this is to do it in the oven. So: pour the water into a roasting dish, add the lime leaves and then the salmon. Cover the dish with foil, put in the oven and cook for about 15 minutes, by which time the salmon should be tender. Remove the dish from the oven and drain the liquid off into a jug. Keep the fish warm simply by replacing the foil on the dish.

Melt the butter in a wide, heavy saucepan that has a tight-fitting lid, and add the oil to stop the butter burning. Soften the onion in the pan and add the spices, then keep cooking till the onion is slightly translucent and suffused with the soft perfume of the spices. Add the rice and stir with a wooden spoon so that it's all well coated. There's not enough onion to give a heavy coating: just make sure the rice is fragrantly slicked.

Pour in the reserved liquid from the jug – about 500ml – and stir before covering with the lid and cooking gently for about 15 minutes. If your stove is vociferous you may need a heat-diffuser.

At the end of the cooking time, when the rice is tender and has lost all chalkiness, turn off the heat, remove the lid, cover the pan with a tea towel and then replace the lid. This will help absorb any extra moisture from the rice. It is also the best way to let the rice stand without getting claggy or cold, which is useful when you've got a few friends and a few dishes to keep your eye on.

Just before you want to eat, drain off any extra liquid that's collected in the dish with the salmon, then flake the fish with a fork. Add to it the rice, eggs, coriander, lime juice and a drop or two of fish sauce. Stir gently to mix – I use a couple of wooden paddles or spatulas – and taste to see if you want any more lime juice or fish sauce. Sprinkle over the zest from the two juiced halves of the lime and serve. I love it served just as it is in the roasting dish, but if you want to, and I often do (consistency is a requirement of a recipe but not a cook), decant into a large plate before you add the lime zest, then surround with lime segments and add the zest and a small handful of freshly chopped coriander.

This is one of those rare dishes that manages to be comforting and light at the same time. And – should you have leftovers, which I wouldn't bank on – it's heavenly eaten, as all leftovers demand to be, standing up, straight from the fridge.

Serves 6.

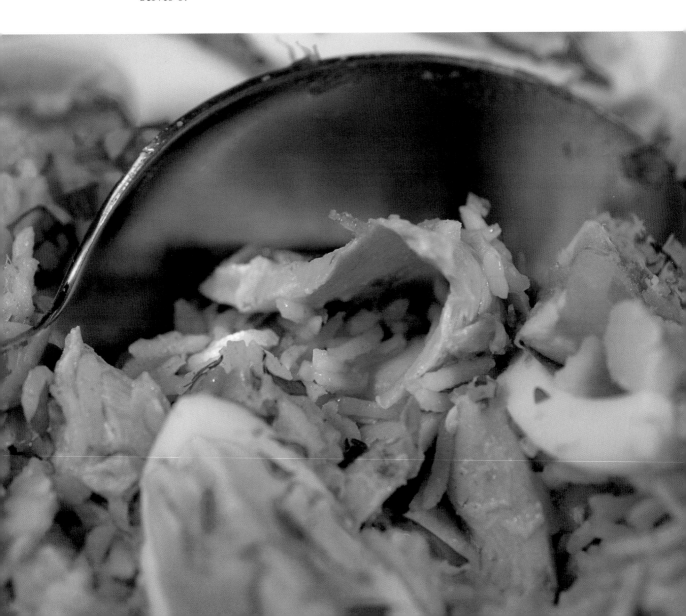

MASALA OMELETTE

Maybe I should come clean here. Although this is a Keralan dish, I have never, in fact, been to Kerala. But the book's designer had just come back from there when we did the pictures for this book and cooked it for us one day. To eat is to be convinced and the omelette found its way into the TV programme. One of the advantages is that it's an unusual thing to eat for breakfast but easy to make, and, what's more, suitable to be cooked for yourself alone. If I'm being honest, I should say that when I cook this for myself, on a weekday at least, I usually dispense with most of the ingredients: I chop two chillies, turn them around in a hot pan with a little bit of oil for a while, then beat them into a couple of eggs, adding some roughly chopped coriander and Maldon salt at the same time. I then pour everything back into the frying pan and cook for a few minutes before sitting the pan under the grill for a top-setting minute or so.

And feel free to add as well as subtract ingredients: grated ginger is good, as is chopped fresh mint or, indeed, dried. You can eat this, flat on the plate, with a knife and fork, or roll it up inside a chapatti that you've just warmed through in the microwave. And don't tell them in Kerala, but I like this with a splodge of brown sauce, too.

1 teaspoon vegetable oil

1 spring onion, sliced finely

1–2 chillies to taste, red or green

1 clove garlic, Microplaned or finely chopped

¼ teaspoon turmeric

1 teaspoon ground coriander

1 teaspoon ground cumin

2 eggs, beaten

freshly chopped coriander for sprinkling over

chapattis to eat with, if you feel like it

Preheat the grill.

Heat the oil in a non-stick frying pan 20–27cm in diameter, and fry the spring onion, chilli, garlic and turmeric until soft. Add the other spices and fry for another minute, stirring occasionally, then add the beaten eggs, swirling the pan to help the eggs set underneath.

When the omelette is nearly set, flash it under the hot grill to finish it off, and serve with chapattis, and fresh coriander or the Green Coriander Chutney which follows.

Serves 1.

GREEN CORIANDER CHUTNEY

This green and fragrant ointment, for all that it's called a chutney, is perfect, both spiky and, strangely, aromatically cooling with the omelette, to be dolloped on the side of the plate or smeared onto an encircling chapati. I first came across a version of it, some time ago, in Claudia Roden's wonderful book of Jewish food; it's rather poetically a dish of the Jews of India. The main bit of fiddling I've done is to replace the vinegar she stipulates with lime juice. It is deeply gorgeous and takes a minute or so to make. I keep whatever's left over in the fridge but the coconut will harden and thicken there; so remember to take it out to get to room temperature before serving it again. You'll probably need to whizz it up in the processor again adding a little more lime juice as you do so, too.

The creamed coconut comes in butter-sized slabs and lasts for ages, so you can keep some in a cupboard, on standby. But to be frank, I've never had any difficulty finding it; I even buy it at my local corner shop.

1–5 green chillies according to taste deseeded and chopped roughly	**1 large bunch of coriander approx. 200g**
2½ cm piece ginger, peeled and roughly chopped	**4 sprigs of mint, de-stalked**
4 garlic cloves	**½ teaspoon salt**
75g creamed coconut	**pinch of caster sugar**
	the juice of 3 limes

Put the chillies, ginger, garlic and creamed coconut into a food processor and blitz to a paste. Add the coriander and mint and pulse again until the herbs blend. Add the salt and pinch of sugar then, with the motor running, pour the juice of two and a half limes down the funnel, processing again to mix thoroughly. Taste to see if you want the juice of the remaining half lime.

Put whatever remains into a jar, and keep it in the fridge for up to a month. As I've said, it will solidify, but this is easily righted.

BLOODY MARY – A JUGFUL

Bloody Mary is the girl for me. A late-morning breakfast, one that oozes into lunch and then into late afternoon, needs liquid accompaniment, and this is what I'd always choose. I steep dried chilli peppers in a bottle of vodka to use just for Bloody Mary, but you don't have to be as extravagantly specialist.

A friend of mine who once worked as a barman in Hong Kong introduced me to the trick of adding a little dry sherry to the mix, and I gladly pass it on to you now.

**300ml chilli vodka (or ordinary vodka
    and a few splashes tabasco)**
splash dry sherry
600ml tomato juice, chilled
**juice of a quarter to half a lemon (to
    taste)**

few shakes of celery salt
few dashes Worcestershire sauce
good sprinkling of Maldon salt, to taste
celery stick or two

Pour all the ingredients, except for the celery sticks, into a jug and use a stick to stir, then leave it in the jug: Bloody Mary needs a stir before each pouring.

Makes approximately 3 half-pint glasses, so be prepared to replenish.

APPLE AND BLACKBERRY KUCHEN

Kuchen may be simply 'cake' in German, but what it means in America, taken there by German refugees, is a sweet, but not too sweet, yeasted dough, baked in a slab and topped as desired with fruit, nuts, or both or neither – to be eaten at breakfast or any time with a cup of coffee. This version has a slightly Anglo-taste: apple and blackberry with a buttery crumble topping. It's unquestionably good as is, but you might consider dolloping over some Greek yoghurt as you eat.

If making yeast dough at breakfast time seems unfathomably demanding, relax in the knowledge that you can make this before you go to bed in the evening, leaving it to rise slowly in the fridge overnight. That way, all you need to do in the morning is pre-heat the oven, take the dough out of the fridge, let it get to room temperature, then knock it back and press it out over the tin, following on from there.

for the cake base:
350–400g strong white flour
½ teaspoon salt
50g caster sugar
½ packet easy-blend yeast
  (about 3g)
2 eggs
½ teaspoon vanilla extract
grated zest of half a lemon
¼ teaspoon ground cinnamon
125ml lukewarm milk
50g butter, softened
30 x 20cm Swiss-roll tin

for the topping:
1 egg beaten with a tablespoon of
  cream and a pinch of ground cinnamon
1 small or ½ medium Bramley apple
  (approx. 175g in weight)
375g blackberries
zest of ½ lemon
50g self-raising flour
25g ground almonds
¼ teaspoon ground cinnamon
50g cold unsalted butter, diced
2 tablespoons caster sugar
2 tablespoons demerara sugar
25g flaked almonds

Put 350g of the flour in a bowl with the salt, sugar and easy-blend yeast. In another bowl, beat the eggs and add them, with the vanilla extract, lemon zest and cinnamon, to the lukewarm milk. Stir the liquid ingredients into the dry ingredients to make a medium-soft dough, being prepared to add more flour as necessary. I generally use about 400g in all, but advise you to start off with the smaller amount: just add more as needed. Work in the soft butter and knead by hand for about 10 minutes or half that time by machine. When the dough is ready it will appear smoother and springier. It suddenly seems to plump up into glossy life.

Cover with a tea towel and leave till doubled in size (an hour to an hour and a quarter). Or leave to rise slowly in a cold place overnight. Then punch down and press to line a Swiss-roll tin measuring 30 x 20cm. You may think it's never going to stretch to fill, but it will, although you may need to let it rest for 10 minutes or so mid-stretch, especially if the dough has had a cold rise. When it's pressed out on the tin, leave it to prove for 15–20 minutes then brush with the egg and cream mixture.

Meanwhile, preheat the oven to 200°C/gas mark 6. Peel and chop the apple and toss it in a bowl with the blackberries and the zest from the other half lemon. Set aside in the bowl for the few minutes it takes to make the crumble topping. Put the flour, ground almonds and cinnamon in a medium-sized bowl, stir to combine, then add the cold, diced butter. Using the tips of your fingers – index and middle stroking the fleshy pads of your thumbs – rub it into the flour. Stop when you have a mixture that resembles clumpy (this is a *very* buttery mixture) porridge oats. Fork in the sugars and flaked almonds.

Tumble the fruit over the egg-washed dough and then sprinkle the crumble on top of that. Put in the oven for 15 minutes, then turn down to 180°C/gas mark 4 and cook for a further 20 minutes or so, until the dough is swelling and golden at its billowing edges and the crumble is set; don't expect it to be crunchy.

Remove from the oven and, if you can, wait five minutes or so before cutting it into greed-satisfying slabs.

Serves 8.

NOTES

NOTES

CHAPTER TWO

COMFORT FOOD

If I'm being honest, for me all food is comfort food, but there are times when you need a bowlful of something hot or a slice of something sweet just to make you feel that the world is a safer place. We all get tired, stressed, sad or lonely, and this is the food that soothes.

MASHED POTATO

No, I haven't gone mad, thinking you need a recipe for mashed potato, it's just that I couldn't even broach the subject of comfort food without starting off here. Plus, there are pointers, suggestions I want to make to ease the labour involved. The first is, buy a potato ricer. It's a cheap, hand-held contraption with a punctured base and a lid that you press down. You put the cooked potato in, squeeze, and out come white worms of fluffy mash – as you can see. The beauty is that you don't need to peel the potato. The skin, or most of it – and you can pick up the few straggly bits that get through the net – stays inside the ricer. Otherwise, if it's a necessary bowl of mashed potato just for one that you're after, I suggest you bake the potatoes (Marfona are best here) for 1–1½ hours at 220°C/gas mark 7 and then just scrape out the flesh and fork it fluffy in a bowl with the milk and butter: greater expenditure on fuel but very little in effort. Plus you get to eat the crunchy skins: divine with a good sprinkling of Maldon salt and a dribble of extra-virgin olive oil.

Mashed potato always seems to taste best if the milk or cream you add to it is warm; I just stick a jug in the microwave with the milk and butter and heat for a minute or so and then pour in while beating. And even if you're using a potato ricer, you do need to beat. A wooden spoon will do: the point is you need to get air into it.

I hesitate before giving quantities, so please regard the specifications below as the merest guidelines. This is about how much you need per person, but then, I would not be appalled to eat a bowl of mash myself made from 500g raw weight of potatoes. It may well be, too, that you don't like your mashed potato as buttery and creamy as I do; I have learnt that there are many people with more austere tastes than mine, though I'm not sure here is the place to indulge them. And – as seems to be the rule with cooking – the more people you have eating, the less per head they seem to need.

250–350g potato, such as Maris Piper or
  King Edward, per person
approx. 75g warm full-fat milk or cream

approx. 50g unsalted butter
salt and pepper, preferably white
freshly grated nutmeg

Boil the halved or chunked (but unpeeled) potatoes in a large pan of salted water. When they are soft enough to mash, drain them thoroughly then push the potato pieces through a potato ricer.

With a wooden spoon, beat in the warm milk or cream and butter and season with salt, pepper and some freshly grated nutmeg to taste. Eat alone and straight from the bowl, for the quintessential comfort food.

SALMON FISHCAKES

This is one of the most comforting suppers I know and has the great virtue of being both a storecupboard standby and a useful way of using leftover mashed potato. A useful way, too, of using up cold boiled potatoes – just push them through the masher and proceed as normal. If the mashed potato has been very buttery and soft to start with they will be harder to mould, but not impossible; you may just find you need to give a sturdier coating of matzo meal before frying. Talking of which, I often do this somewhat differently than specified below: I make the patties, then freeze them (on a clingfilmed baking sheet) until hard, then bag them up; when I want to eat them, I dip them, stonily unthawed, into the egg and matzo meal, fry them on both sides in hot oil until golden and then sit them on kitchen towel in a baking tray in an oven preheated to 120°C/gas mark ½ for about 40 minutes or until warmed through. And you could leave them here for about 3 hours without doing any damage.

The reason I use matzo meal rather than breadcrumbs is that I find bought breadcrumbs horrible and I am presuming that for an undemanding recipe like this you are not going to want to plan ahead and busy yourself making them from fresh. Matzo meal is now anyway widely available at supermarkets, and well worth keeping in store. And I use tinned salmon here because I think, strangely enough, that's how they taste best (if it's good enough for Marguerite Costa, it's good enough for me) and it means you can have the wherewithal for these about the place at all times. I do have to warn, though, that, the unfried mixture smells absolutely vile. Just hold on to the thought that, once cooked, it tastes wonderful. And with these fat bronzed coral slabs, I suggest frozen peas and tomato ketchup. I don't even like tomato ketchup much but just as with shepherd's pie, it's an essential here.

for the fishcakes:
350–500g cold mashed potato
418g tinned salmon, preferably organic
15g unsalted butter, melted (if the
   mashed potato hasn't got any butter
   in it)
fat pinch cayenne pepper
grated zest of ½ lemon

salt and pepper
1 egg

for coating and frying:
2 eggs
100g matzo meal, preferably medium
50g unsalted butter
2 tablespoons vegetable oil

In a large bowl, and preferably with your hands, mix together all the fishcake ingredients.

Cover a baking sheet with clingfilm, plunge your hands back into the mixture and form fat, palm-sized patties. Place these on the baking sheet and stand in the fridge to firm up for about 20 minutes to an hour – or considerably longer if that helps.

Beat the eggs in a shallow soup bowl and sprinkle the matzo meal onto a dinner plate. One by one, dip the fishcakes into the beaten egg and then into the matzo meal, sprinkling and dredging over as you go to help coat them. When you're all done, put the butter and oil in a large frying pan, heat till it begins to fizzle and then fry the fishcakes on each side until the crusts are golden, and speckled brown in parts, and the soothing centres are warmed through.

Makes 7–9 x 7cm-diameter fishcakes.

DOUBLE POTATO AND HALLOUMI BAKE

I first made this for a piece I was writing for *Vogue* on the mood-enhancing properties of carbohydrates, as promoted by such books as – and how's this for a title? – *Potatoes not Prozac*. The fact that shortly after filing the article I went on a low-carbohydrate diet should not worry us too much here, for I should say that no one has eaten this without being mad for it. It's a simple idea, and as simple to execute. What's more, there's a balance between the components – bland and sweet potatoes, almost-caramelised onion and garlic, more juicy sweetness with the peppers and then the uncompromising plain saltiness of the halloumi (which you should be able to get easily in a supermarket) – that seems to add to the eater's equilibrium in turn. You could substitute feta, or do without the cheese altogether if you wanted to serve this as a side dish to roast chicken, say, but in which case be generous with the Maldon salt once the bake comes out of the oven.

And forgetting about pseudo-scientific and other optimistic theories for a while; this is so upliftingly beautiful to look at: real good-mood colours.

- 1 large sweet potato, the orange-fleshed American variety
- 1 large Desirée potato or other red/firm potato
- 1 red onion
- 1 yellow pepper
- 1 red pepper
- ½ head of garlic
- 4 tablespoons olive oil
- black pepper
- 125g halloumi cheese, sliced as thinly as you can
- ovenproof baking dish, 25 x 15cm

Preheat the oven to 200°C/gas mark 6.

Cut the sweet potato into rough 4cm cubes and the Desirée slightly smaller (2½cm) as the sweet potato will cook more quickly. Halve the red onion, then cut each half into 4–6 segments, discarding any tough outer skin. De-seed the peppers and cut into 2½cm squares, and separate the cloves of garlic. Put everything into a large roasting tin or whatever you want to use (it should be big, otherwise use two dishes) and, using your hands, give the vegetables a good coating of olive oil. Season with black pepper, but no salt as the cheese will make it salty (and anyway, the salt will make water leech out). Cook for 45 minutes, by which time the vegetables should be cooked through and here and there tinged with brown. You'll need to turn the oven up to maximum or light the grill for the endgame: so place the thinly sliced cheese on top of the bake, and put it back in the very hot oven or under the grill until the cheese has melted and turned slightly brown on top, about 5–10 minutes. Serve straight out of the roasting tin.

Serves 2–3.

CHICKEN SOUP AND KNEIDLACH

Yes, this is quite a palaver to make (although it's time-consuming rather than laborious, which is a significant distinction) but there is nothing more comforting to eat. This isn't tribal sentiment; for all that it's known as Jewish Penicillin, I wasn't raised on it, but eating it makes me feel I should have been, that indeed we all should have been. (That scientists have recently found chicken broth to contain anti-inflammatory and anti-bacterial properties is interesting for those on the lookout for non-patented flu remedies, but true believers – culinary as much as devotional – never needed any such corroboration.)

What we ate at home, rather, was boiled chicken with rice, and I suppose for that reason I like rice in the soup, if it's to have anything – though it truly is at its best as a pure, gold, soothing liquid. But actually it is traditional to sully its purity with starch: go for *lokshen* (vermicelli) or go native with *kneidlach*, which are best described as cracker-meal dumplings. I always used to think that in order to appreciate these you really needed to have been brought up on them. I wasn't and remained resistant. But I've since found that they do not have to be the digestion-challenging cannonballs that tradition all but decrees. (Not, you understand, that stodge, in this context, is exactly bad.) Just make sure to whisk the egg well before adding the other ingredients and what you come up with are toothsome dumplings that are soothingly fluffy as well as comfortingly substantial. So I'm happy to give you my friend Olivia Lichtenstein's recipe for them and urge you to get mixing and rolling. The fat used should be *schmalz* (chicken fat), which will be available at any kosher butcher's; failing that – dietary laws considered – it should be goose fat or margarine. But at the risk of offending the laws of Leviticus – and forget risk, it's a dead cert here – I use butter. But, you know, schmalz is not hard to make: just pluck out the gobbets of chicken fat that cluster just inside the cavity and melt them in a small pan over low heat. That should be more than enough to provide the two tablespoons required here.

As for the chicken in your pot: it really has to be a boiler. A boiling chicken yields up flavour like nothing else, and its flesh needs long cooking, so it doesn't go stringy after hours of boiling. If you can't get hold of a boiling chicken, then you'll have to use a roasting one, but don't cook it for more than an hour and a half. You can then take the meat off the bones, put the carcass back in the stock and carry on cooking it, though you may still need to bump up the flavour; in which case, I'd recommend a glug or two of Benedicta's Touch of Taste Concentrated Chicken Bouillon.

For some reason, chicken soup seems to get hotter than any other liquid known to humankind: unless you're careful, you'll sear your throat before you soothe it. But soothe it you truly will: this is amazingly restorative stuff.

2 small or 1 large boiling chicken	a few stalks of parsley
1 unpeeled onion, halved	a few peppercorns
1 stick celery	2 bay leaves
2 carrots, peeled and chunked	1 tablespoon salt

Put all the ingredients in a large stockpot, cover abundantly with water, and bring to the boil. Skim to remove all the grey scum that will float to the surface, then let cook at a simmer for about 3 hours. Just keep tasting: when the broth tastes golden and chickeny, it's ready. Remove the chicken and, if you like, leave the soup to get cold so you can remove any fat that collects on the surface. That way you accrue some schmalz, too.

Reheat the stock, and serve it as a plain soup, or add a few carrot batons – from about 2 carrots, say – and cook in the soup, adding some torn up pieces of chicken to warm through at the end. I like to add freshly chopped parsley.

Serves 4 (or 8 Gentiles).

KNEIDLACH

As I said, schmalz you'll have to get from a kosher butcher unless you can render or skim enough from the chicken above, but matzo meal is available at supermarkets (I prefer to use the medium rather than the fine ground). It's worth trying these dumplings at least once: there are days when only stodge will do. And, to be fair, made properly, these aren't heavy so much as dense: I am relying on your charity to appreciate the distinction here.

1 egg	3 tablespoons water or soup stock
30g schmalz, margarine or butter,	100g medium matzo meal
melted	pinch of salt and a grind of pepper

Whisk the egg in a large-ish bowl, then whisk in the melted schmalz (or whatever). Carry on whisking as you add the water or soup stock, the matzo meal and salt and pepper, and mix together into a rough paste; if it's too stiff to feel that it might be malleable later, add a little more water. Put in the fridge to chill for an hour (or leave overnight if you wish) then dig out small lumps of paste and roll them into walnut-sized balls between the palms of your hands. Cook the kneidlach in boiling, salted water and simmer for about 40 minutes (you can just cook them directly in the soup, but I'll do anything to preserve its unstarchy clearness). They are cooked when they rise to the surface. Add to the soup, and ladle out generously into waiting bowls. The etiquette here is, when people have the spoon halfway towards their mouth, before they've even had one spoonful, and therefore have yet to exclaim about how wonderful it is, to ask, querulously, 'It's all right? Is there anything wrong?' while sighing longsufferingly.

Makes about 20.

LEMON RISOTTO

This is comfort food on so many levels. For one, risotto has to be one of the most comforting things to eat ever. What's more, although everyone goes on about the finicketiness and crucial fine-tuning involved, I find risotto immensely comforting to make: in times of strain, mindless repetitive activity – in this case, 20 minutes of stirring – can really help. What you don't want to do is make risotto for large numbers of people, which is why I've indicated that this serves two (as supper in its entirety); if you want to call it into service as a starter, then reckon on its feeding four.

There is a more personal reason why this is comforting for me. The recipe comes from Anna del Conte (from her *Secrets of an Italian Kitchen* to be exact) and she, beyond any doubt the best Italian foodwriter around, is the person I turn to for bolstering and solace. Just reading her books provides instant, essential nourishment.

2 shallots

1 stick of celery

60g unsalted butter

1 tablespoon olive oil

300g risotto rice, preferably Vialone
   Nano

1 litre vegetable stock (I use Marigold
   stock powder)

zest and juice of ½ unwaxed lemon

needles from 2 small sprigs of fresh
   rosemary, finely chopped

1 egg yolk

60ml (4 tablespoons) grated parmesan,
   plus more to sprinkle

60ml (4 tablespoons) double cream

Maldon salt to taste

good grating pepper, preferably white

Put the shallots and celery into a Magimix and blitz until they are a finely chopped mush. Heat half the butter, the oil and the shallot and celery mixture in a wide saucepan, and cook to soften the mixture for about 5 minutes, making sure it doesn't catch. Mix in the rice, stirring to give it a good coating of oil and butter. Meanwhile, heat the stock in another saucepan and keep it at simmering point.

Pour a ladleful of the stock into the rice and keep stirring until the stock is absorbed. Then add another ladleful and stir again. Continue doing this until the rice is al dente. You may not need all of the stock, equally, you may need to add hot water from the kettle.

Mix the lemon zest and the rosemary into the risotto, and in a small bowl beat the egg yolk, lemon juice, parmesan, cream and pepper.

When the risotto is ready – when the rice is no longer chalky, but still has some bite – take it off the heat and add the bowl of eggy, lemony mixture, and the remaining butter and salt to taste. Serve with more grated parmesan if you wish, check the seasoning and dive in.

Serves 2.

STOVETOP RICE PUDDING FOR EMERGENCIES

For those days when you just can't wait the three hours for a proper, old-fashioned rice pudding, this is what you need. In fact, it's just a sweet risotto, with warm milk substituted for the stock. This does mean that the rice takes longer to cook – and what's more, you want it rather less al dente than is usually desirable – but it's the best I can offer. Anyway, you can't, on eating this, resent one moment of your stoveside-stirring captivity.

700ml full-fat milk

1 heaped tablespoon unsalted butter

2–3 tablespoons caster sugar or vanilla sugar

60g (about 4 tablespoons) risotto rice, preferably Vialone Nano

½ teaspoon good vanilla extract (if not using vanilla sugar)

2–3 tablespoons double cream, the thicker and fattier the better

Heat the milk in a pan that preferably has a lip, which will make pouring easier (or give it a couple of minutes in a plastic jug in the microwave). When it's about to boil (but don't let it) turn off the flame. Melt the butter and a tablespoonful of the sugar in a heavy-based pan. When hissing away in a glorious pale caramelly pool, add the rice and stir to coat stickily. Gradually add the milk, stirring the rice all the time, and letting each swoosh of milk get absorbed into the consequently swelling rice before adding the next bit. To see when it's ready, start tasting at 20 minutes, but be prepared to go on for 35. You may want to add more milk, too (and if the rice tastes cooked before all the milk's absorbed, don't use all of it).

When the rice feels as it should, thick and sticky and creamy, take it off the heat, and beat in another tablespoonful of sugar (taste and see if you want yet more), the vanilla, if using, and as much of the cream as you like. Think of this as the *mantecatura*: the final addition to a risotto, to thicken and add fat-globular volume, normally of butter and grated parmesan; indeed just add butter if you haven't got any cream in the house.

Serves 1.

CHOCOLATE FUDGE CAKE

I have a bad Amazon habit. You know the 'when the going gets tough, the tough go shopping' line? Well, the not-so-tough get their retail therapy online. Or I do: when I can't sleep I start ordering books. And I comfort myself twice over by telling myself how useful they are, how they really help my work. I offer this recipe, adapted from a book that in itself soothes, *Tish Boyle's Diner Desserts*, bought at about 3am one unravellingly wakeful night, as proof.

This is the sort of cake you'd want to eat the whole of when you'd been chucked. But even the sight of it, proud and tall and thickly iced on its stand, comforts.

for the cake:
400g plain flour
250g golden caster sugar
100g light muscovado sugar
50g best quality cocoa powder
2 teaspoons baking powder
1 teaspoon bicarbonate of soda
½ teaspoon salt
3 eggs
142ml/small tub sour cream
1 tablespoon vanilla extract

175g unsalted butter, melted and cooled
125ml corn oil
300ml chilled water

for the fudge icing:
175g dark chocolate, minimum 70% cocoa solids
250g unsalted butter, softened
275g icing sugar, sifted
1 tablespoon vanilla extract

Preheat the oven to 180°C/gas mark 4.

Butter and line the bottom of two 20cm sandwich tins.

In a large bowl, mix together the flour, sugars, cocoa, baking powder, bicarb and salt. In another bowl or wide-necked measuring jug whisk together the eggs, sour cream and vanilla until blended. Using a freestanding or handheld electric mixer, beat together the melted butter and corn oil until just blended (you'll need another large bowl for this if using the hand whisk; the freestanding mixer comes with its own bowl), then beat in the water. Add the dry ingredients all at once and mix together on a slow speed. Add the egg mixture, and mix again until everything is blended and then pour into the prepared tins. And actually, you could easily do this manually; I just like my toys and find the KitchenAid a comforting presence in itself.

Bake the cakes for 50–55 minutes, or until a cake-tester comes out clean. Cool the cakes in their tins on a wire rack for 15 minutes, and then turn the cakes out onto the rack to cool completely.

To make the icing, melt the chocolate in the microwave – 2–3 minutes on medium should do it – or in a bowl sitting over a pan of simmering water, and let cool slightly.

In another bowl beat the butter until it's soft and creamy (again, I use the KitchenAid here) and then add the sieved icing sugar and beat again until everything's light and fluffy. I know sieving is a pain, the one job in the kitchen I really hate, but you have to do it or the icing will be unsoothingly lumpy. Then gently add the vanilla and chocolate and mix together until everything is glossy and smooth.

Sandwich the middle of the cake with about a quarter of the icing, and then ice the top and sides too, spreading and smoothing with a rubber spatula.

Serves 10. Or 1 with a broken heart.

NOTES

NOTES

CHAPTER THREE

TV DINNERS

Even if you like cooking, at the end of a long day you don't necessarily have much time or energy for it. Of course you can always phone for a pizza, but I find that a bit of stoveside pottering helps me unwind. What I'm talking about here is the food you can cook on those days when you just have to hit the kitchen running…

MOZZARELLA IN CARROZZA

This is Italian food before Tuscan rustic chic. The 'in carrozza' bit means 'in a carriage' and doesn't really explain what this golden-crusted fried mozzarella sandwich is about, just gives an indication that the milky cheese is somehow contained. What you should know if you've never tried it (apart from the fact that it is one of the easiest, most gratifying laptop dinners imaginable) is that it is somewhere between eggy bread, cheese on toast and fried slice. For children (and do bear this in mind for a quick, hot filler when they get back from school) it is desirably like pizza sandwich, and could be made more so with tomato sauce smeared within the bread's tender interior.

It works, as well, served with a tomato or, for adults, chilli sauce alongside, into which you can dip the corners of the oozing sandwich as you eat. And, unorthodox though this is, I love it with a fierce sprinkling of chopped fresh red chilli in with, and to counter, the gorgeously melting blandness of the mozzarella.

I can't pretend this version is absolutely authentic: it wasn't invented using plastic white bread. But white sliced is just fine, and, frankly, what I use. For one thing, if you have children it's what you tend to have in the house. Just be sure to use the lightest hand when dunking it in the milk; more than a moment and the bread will have dissolved into unredeemable mushiness. But don't be cautious about this: it's quick and easy to make, and requires very little in the way of shopping. Speaking of which, it is not worth buying the better, and more expensive, buffalo mozzarella here. The milky dampness of that cheese is not required; it is anyway too liquid and, besides, ordinary cow's-milk mozzarella produces just the right fleshy goo, oozing out of the cut sandwich into stringy, chewy ribbons.

6 slices white bread, crusts removed

1 ball mozzarella, cut into approx. half-
  centimetre slices, then strips

125ml full-fat milk

3 heaped tablespoons plain (or better
  still Italian 00) flour

1 egg

salt and pepper

olive oil (not extra-virgin) for frying

Make sandwiches out of the bread and mozzarella, leaving a little margin around the edges unfilled with cheese, and press the edges together with your fingers to help seal. (One of the advantages of plastic bread is that it is easily wodged together.) Pour the milk into one soup bowl, the flour into another, and beat the egg with salt and pepper in another. Warm the oil in a frying pan over a medium heat. Dunk the sandwiches briefly, one by one, in the milk, then dredge in the flour, then dip in the beaten egg. Fry in hot oil on each side till crisp and gold and remove to kitchen towel. Cut in half and apply to face.

  Serves 2.

CHICKEN WITH CHORIZO AND CANNELLINI

This may sound a kind of fancy thing to be making at the end of a working day, but it is fabulously easy, fabulously quick and everything can be bought at a quick supermarket stop in your lunch hour. Yes, chicken stock is itemised, but I use 500ml of boiling water to which I've added a tablespoonful or so of Benedicta Touch of Taste Concentrated Chicken Bouillon – one of my storecupboard standbys. If you can't find proper chorizo sausages – the kind that are sold in 200g loops (though I get it from my local Sainsbury's with no difficulty) – then buy 100g of slicing chorizo (the salame kind) in one chunk, and then chop it up into small chunks yourself. And don't worry in the slightest if instead of sprinkling over sweet, smoked paprika at the end, you just use the ordinary kind.

And don't agonize over the chicken cut either. I like to use a supreme (a skinless breast portion with the peg-bone still attached) but a regular breast portion would do just fine. Any firm white fish (just replace the chicken stock with fish stock) would be wonderful here too instead of the chicken and – as further speed-conscious inducement – would need only about 3 minutes' poaching. Finally, the chorizo and cannellini beans, without any further adornment, are pretty damn good, too. Worth bearing in mind as a way of sprucing up any leftover cold cuts that otherwise stare reproachfully out at you from their fridge-bound, clingfilmed confinement.

500ml chicken stock (see left)

1 free-range chicken supreme
  (or skinless breast portion)

approx. 125g trimmed kale (sold in
  250g packets)

1–2 teaspoons olive oil (not extra-virgin)

100g chorizo, sliced then chopped

410g tin cannellini beans, drained

smoked sweet paprika for sprinkling

In a saucepan, bring the stock to a gentle boil, lower in the chicken portion and cook, still gently, for 10 minutes or until all trace of pink has disappeared. Pierce with the point of a knife to check.

Meanwhile, cook the kale, which you've roughly torn into pieces, in boiling salted water for about 5 minutes (if it's tough) and drain. Then heat the oil in a frying pan, throw in the chopped chorizo, add the drained cannellini and, stirring, warm everything through, moistening with a couple of tablespoons or so of the chicken stock – or more if you want this soupier.

Tip the beans and chorizo into a shallow bowl or lipped plate, roughly arrange the kale on top (drizzling with a little extra-virgin olive oil if you like) and then lift the cooked chicken out of the stock with a spatula or fish slice and sit this on top of the kale ruff. Sprinkle the pale chicken breast with the paprika and gaze at your Spanish still life of a supper before eating it.

Serves 1.

LINGUINE WITH GARLIC OIL AND PANCETTA

Three ingredients: one great supper. I like this greedily mounded in a bowl and taken up to bed to be eaten, or rather shovelled in, in front of the television. But that's not obligatory.

Good pancetta is not found everywhere (check out butcher's and delicatessen's) so it makes sense, when you buy it, to get a few 250g blocks. Freeze them separately then just take each one out of the deep-freeze in the morning and return after work to have this fat-striped slab of Italian bacon ready and at your disposal in the evening. Otherwise, you could buy a packet of lardons – those diced bacon cubes – from the supermarket or even use ordinary bacon, snipped into straggly bits. Just bear in mind that cut-up bacon will not need more than about 5 minutes in the hot, aromatic fat to cook.

Of course you could cook the pancetta or bacon in a frying pan, but why I like using the oven is that it needs no supervision. You can put the pancetta in the oven, put the pasta in the boiling, salted water, go up and run yourself a bath (taking your timer with you) and then come down and just drain and toss and dinner's made.

And naturally you can use whatever pasta you like, it's just that linguine (a long pasta that's wider than spaghetti and thicker than tagliatelle) is my favourite – a good reason, it seems to me, to specify it here.

2 tablespoons garlic-infused olive oil   **250g linguine**
250g pancetta

Preheat the oven to 240°C/gas mark 8.

Fill a large saucepan with water and bring to the boil. While it's heating up, put the garlic olive oil in an ovenproof dish; I use an enamel Le Creuset one, measuring 30 x 20cm. Remove the rind from the pancetta and put it in the dish (to render down: you want as much bacony juices as possible) then dice the rest of the pancetta and add these cubes to the oil, smooshing them about with your fingers to make sure they're equally, if lightly, coated. When the water's boiling, put the dish of garlic-oiled pancetta in the oven then salt the boiling water and add the linguine; these should need about 10 minutes to cook. When the pasta's ready, drain it, reserving a scant cupful of the cooking water and take the pancetta dish out of the oven. Tip the drained linguine into the dish and toss well, adding some of the pasta-cooking water, drop by cautious drop, for lubrication as you need it.

And that's it: I like this without parmesan, but a sprinkling of roughly scissored parsley, should you feel inclined, is always a good idea.

Serves 2.

SALT AND PEPPER SQUID

Just because something's unfamiliar doesn't mean it's hard to cook. OK, I understand that when you think 'TV dinner', squid is hardly the first thing to come to mind, but I am asking you to think again. This is unexpectedly easy to shop for as well as easy to cook. Baby squid (better here than tougher, grown-up, windsock-sized ones) can be found, frozen, in 500g boxes, to be stashed in your freezer and thawed as needed. And while any recipe that involves a pestle and mortar can seem like too much kitchen faffing when you get back from work, let me tell you that a bit of murderous bashing can be a great stress-relieving exercise. But if you're not convinced (and believe me I understand: until recently I had only to read the words 'pestle and mortar' to be filled with dread and intimidation) you can always use one of those little electric coffee-bean or spice grinders for blitzing the salt and pepper. Already-ground pepper and fine salt is not an impossible option; I won't pretend they'll be as good, but as long as you don't use that school-pepper-container dust – more sneeze-powder than aromatic spice – it'll be just fine.

approx. 500ml groundnut oil (to come about 1cm up in a frying pan)

2 tablespoons Maldon salt

2 tablespoons black peppercorns

75g cornflour

500g baby squid, cut into rings, tentacles left unchopped

lemon for squeezing

Put the oil in a frying pan over a high heat. Bash the salt and peppercorns in a pestle and mortar till a bit more than bruised but not quite pulverised, and combine this mixture in a freezer bag with the cornflour, adding the squid and tossing to coat well but not heavily.

When the oil's very hot – not quite smoking but nearly – fry the squid (knocking any excess cornflour back in the bag first) in batches (about four, probably) and cook each batch for about a minute or so till just crisp on the outside and still sweet and tender within. You probably won't need to turn the squid since the oil should bubble up and cook both sides at once, but do if you feel better. Remove to plates lined with kitchen towel. After the squid's sat for about half a minute, remove the greasy towel – though sometimes, I dispense with this faddy stage – squeeze lemon over and eat with your fingers – quickly.

Serves 2.

THAI YELLOW PUMPKIN AND SEAFOOD CURRY

I use the term 'TV dinners' loosely. Not everything in this chapter is written with sofa-bound slumping in mind. It's also a good idea to have something up your sleeve that you can cook quickly, and simply, when you've got friends coming over to supper midweek after work. This is that something. Don't let the length of the list of ingredients put you off. You really could go to the supermarket at lunchtime and buy everything you need. What's more, most of it keeps: salmon, raw prawns, lime leaves and lemongrass in the deep-freeze (and all but the salmon can be used from frozen); curry paste in the fridge; the coconut milk, fish sauce, fish-stock concentrate and turmeric in the cupboard. In other words, one shopping expedition, many curries.

Yes, the coriander you'll need to buy fresh (though at a push you could buy a box of already chopped frozen stuff) as you will the pumpkin and pak choi and – give or take – lime, but whatever, you have the base here for a number of curries. Once you've cooked this and seen both how simple and how divine it is, you'll see how you can adapt it for different produce.

You have to have rice with curry and the simplest way to cook this is to get an electric rice cooker. The best part of this is that once you've put the rice and water in, the rice cooks itself and – with my model at least – stays warm for 12 hours, so you're not going to have to do any last-minute timing shenanigans. You just stick the rice on when you get in, and it'll be fine whatever time people bowl up for dinner. With the same idea in mind, you should know that you can cook the curry up till the part where the pumpkin is tender and then leave it, reheating it later to cook (for all of about 3 minutes) the prawns and salmon. Given that most people are late for dinner when they're coming after work, this means that you don't have the dilemma of either leaving something spoiling on the stove or having a frenzied bout of last-minute cooking once they arrive.

I've said 1–2 tablespoons of curry paste. This is because pastes vary enormously in their strengths and people vary enormously in their tastes. Some like it hot: I like it very hot – and use 2 tablespoonfuls. But it might be wiser to add 1 tablespoonful first and then taste later, once all the liquid's in, to see if you want to add more.

One last bossy note: if you can't get raw prawns, don't use cooked ones; just double the amount of salmon.

400ml tin coconut milk

1–2 tablespoons yellow (or red) Thai curry paste

350ml fish stock (I use boiling water and a slug of Benedicta Touch of Taste Concentrated Fish Bouillon; cubes would do)

3 tablespoons fish sauce

2 tablespoons palm sugar or caster sugar

3 lemongrass stalks, each cut into three and bruised with the flat of a knife

3 lime leaves, de-stalked and cut into strips

½ teaspoon turmeric

1kg pumpkin (or butternut squash), peeled and cut into large-bite-sized chunks

500g salmon fillet, preferably organic, skinned and cut into large, bite-sized chunks

500g peeled raw prawns

pak choi or any other green vegetables of your choice

juice of ½–1 lime, to taste

coriander, to serve

Skim the thick creamy top off the tin of coconut milk and put it, over medium heat, into a large saucepan or casserole with the curry paste. Let it sizzle and, using a fork, whisk or wooden spoon, beat milk and paste together until combined. Still beating gently, add the rest of the coconut milk, fish stock, fish sauce, sugar, lemongrass, lime leaves and turmeric. Bring to a boil and then add the pumpkin. Cook on a fast simmer until the pumpkin is tender, about 15 minutes, although different sorts of pumpkins can vary enormously in the time they take to cook; some squash take as little as 5 minutes.

As I mentioned, you can cook the curry up till this part in advance, maybe leaving the pumpkin with a tiny bit of bite to it (it will soften and cook as the pan cools). Either way, when you're about 5 minutes away from wanting to eat, get ready to cook the seafood.

So, to the robustly simmering pan, add the salmon and prawns (if you're using the prawns from frozen they'll need to go in before the salmon). When the salmon and prawns have cooked through, which shouldn't take more than 3–4 minutes, stir in any green veg you're using – sliced, chopped or shredded as suits – and tamp down with a wooden spoon. When the pak choi's wilted, squeeze in the juice of half a lime, stir and taste and add the juice of the remaining half if you feel it needs it. Take the pan off the heat or decant the curry into a large bowl, and sprinkle over the coriander; the point is that the coriander goes in just before serving. Serve with more chopped coriander for people to add to their own bowls as they eat, and some plain Thai or basmati rice.

Serves 4–6.

BITTER ORANGE ICE CREAM

I know that suggesting homemade ice cream for an easy after-work supper makes me sound as if I'm going into deranged-superwoman overdrive, but may I put the case for the defence?

    All you do to make this is zest and juice some fruit, add icing sugar and cream, whisk and freeze. This requires no stirring or churning and it tastes unlike anything you could buy. So if you've got friends coming over for the curry, above, you can serve this for pudding to amazed admiration without giving yourself anything approaching a hard time. I use my KitchenAid, but a cheap hand-held electric mixer would do fine; and frankly, a hand whisk wouldn't kill you.

    I first made this with Seville oranges, but since these are available only in January here, it would be unhelpfully restricting to suggest no substitutes out of season (though you could always freeze the oranges, either whole or just their zest and juice). I won't lie to you and say that my suggested substitutes are quite as magnificent as the original – nothing can provide that biting, aromatic intensity that you get from Seville oranges, which have the taste of orange and the ravaging sourness of lemons – but ordinary eating oranges combined with lime juice provide a glorious tangy and fragrant hit of their own.

**3 Seville oranges or 1 eating orange
and 2 limes
175g icing sugar**

**large pot (584ml) double cream
wafers to serve (optional)**

If using Seville oranges, grate the zest of 2 of them. Squeeze the juice of all 3 and pour into a bowl with the zest and sugar. If you're going for the sweet orange and lime option, grate the zest of the orange and one of the limes, juice them and add to the sugar as before. Stir to dissolve the sugar and add the double cream.

Whip everything until it holds soft peaks, and then turn into a shallow air-tight container (of approximately 2 litres) with a lid. Cover and freeze until firm (from 3 to 5 hours). Remove to ripen for 15–20 minutes (or 30–40 in the fridge) before eating. Serve in a bowl, in cones, with wafers – however you like.

Serves 6.

NOTES

_____

_____

_____

_____

_____

_____

_____

_____

_____

_____

_____

_____

_____

_____

_____

_____

CHAPTER FOUR

PARTY GIRL

I'd have to go and lie down in a darkened room if I started trying my hand at real party catering, but for children's birthdays or lazily-peopled gatherings in a summer garden, there's always food you can do, and that I regularly return to, that actually makes you feel pleased you invited anyone in the first place.

PIGS IN BLANKETS

As far as I know, Pigs in Blankets is a wartime recipe; I first came across it in an old *Woman's Own* cookery book of my grandmother's, but have noticed differing versions of it since. The original I saw was for a chunky parcel – sausages wrapped in a thick potato pastry and then baked, wonderfully true somehow to the evocative title. This is a simplified version made with a fork-mixed cheese scone dough, and a diminutive one, perfectly suited to a children's birthday party or simply to entertain them in the kitchen.

In fact, I use the cooked pork cocktail sausages from Marks & Spencer's, partly because cooking, cooling, then wrapping sausages seems a palaver and partly because this way I'm less tempted to eat them myself. Somehow, though, I still manage.

Anyway, children love them, and they are reassuringly easy to make. In fact, there's nothing about their preparation that even a modestly interested child couldn't cope with.

375g self-raising flour

1 heaped teaspoon salt

25g grated Red Leicester cheese (or use Cheddar)

250ml full-fat milk

1 egg

3 tablespoons vegetable oil

1 packet of 50 pork cocktail sausages

to glaze:

1 egg, mixed with a dollop of milk and half a teaspoon of salt

Preheat the oven to 220°C/gas mark 7.

Measure the flour into a bowl, add the salt and grated cheese and mix lightly with a fork. Pour the milk into a measuring jug to come up to the 250ml mark and then crack in the egg and add the oil. Beat to combine, then pour into the dry ingredients, forking to mix as you go. You may, at the end, feel the dough's either too dry or too damp: add either more milk or more flour and fork together again till you've got a soft dough that's not too sticky to be rolled out.

Break the dough into two pieces and roll the first one out onto a lightly floured surface. Scone dough is a dream to work with; in fact, I find it deeply pleasurable. Just roll as clumsily and heavy handedly as you like: no harm will come to it. You want a thin, but not exaggeratedly so, rectangle. A square wouldn't be the end of the world either, so don't start getting out the geometry set: this is the roughest of instructions.

Cut the dough into approximately 4cm strips, and then cut each strip at approximately 6cm intervals so that you end up with a collection of small, raggedy oblongs (I just cut each strip as I go, but it's probably more efficient to do the whole batch of dough in one go).

Take a cocktail sausage and put it at one end of an oblong at a slight diagonal and then roll up, pressing on the infinitely compliant dough to squeeze it shut, and then place on a non-stick baking sheet, or one lined with parchment. Carry on until you've finished all your strips and then get to work with the remaining dough. Three baking sheets should do it.

Now, dip a pastry brush into the beaten egg mixture and paint on a golden glaze. Put in the oven and cook for 12–15 minutes, by which time they should be puffy and burnished. Remove from the oven and let cool a little before giving them to the children.

Makes 50.

LILAC- OR CHOCOLATE-TOPPED CUPCAKES

What's a children's party without cupcakes? In truth, it's better to make mini ones for smaller children; they just like the icing anyway, so there's no point in majoring in the sponge. Since we're going through a purple stage at the moment – pink, for us, is *so* last year – I go full out for their garish pleasure by tinting the icing a heart-stopping lilac with a minuscule blob of Grape Violet food-colouring paste. But since adults love cupcakes just as much, I suggest them also as a pudding for a grown-up party – in which case, though, make a chocolate ganache to be smoothed over full-sized cupcakes. In both cases, I decorate with gold buttons, but if you can't find these, a conker-shiny Minstrel, plonked glossily on top, would seduce just as well.

For something a little more festive, in the case of the grown-up ones at least (and as an alternative to a traditional birthday cake), forget the central decoration on top and spike each cupcake with a cake-candle and leave to smoulder atmospherically for a while on serving. And to make chocolate cupcakes, which in either instance could be thought preferable, take out a tablespoonful of flour after weighing and replace with the same amount of cocoa.

for cupcakes:	for icing:
125g self-raising flour	**approx. 350g icing sugar, sieved, or**
125g very soft unsalted butter	**instant royal icing**
125g caster sugar	**food colouring paste**
2 eggs	**gold chocolate buttons (or Minstrels)**
1–2 teaspoons vanilla extract	**12-bun muffin tray or 3 x 12-bun mini-**
few tablespoons full-fat milk	**muffin trays with appropriately sized**
	paper cases

Preheat the oven to 200°C/gas mark 6.

Put all the ingredients for the cupcakes except the milk into a food processor and blitz furiously. Then pour in the milk, and process again until you have a smooth batter. Divide the mixture between either the big muffin tray or the three small trays.

Cook the big muffins for about 15–20 minutes, and the small ones for about 10 minutes, although you might need to keep a closer eye on the little ones. Cool the cupcakes on a wire rack.

To ice the mini-cupcakes mix the icing sugar with a tablespoon or two of water from a recently boiled kettle or cold water (according to packet instructions) for instant royal icing until you have a smooth, spreadable paste. In both cases add water slowly: you don't want this runny and nothing is more irritating than having to start sieving more sugar. The merest, tiniest blob of food-colouring paste – in this case, as I said, Grape Violet – will be enough to bring a dizzy and rich-toned intensity to the proceedings; you can always add more colouring if you want, but again the important thing is to guard against having to do any more sieving. And if you have been too heavy-handed and landed yourself with a batch of unusably dark icing, then just make up some more plain white icing and add to tone down.

Slice any peaking humps off the tops of the cakes with a sharp knife and then pour, from a dunked-in spoon, the icing over each cake until the tops are thickly and smoothly covered. Let stand for a couple of minutes until the icing has set a tiny bit and then dot a gold button or other decoration of your choice on top.

CHOCOLATE GANACHE

This is a very useful icing to have up your sleeve for any sort of cake. The quantities below make enough to ice, thickly and glossily, 12 normal-sized cupcakes, but since all a chocolate ganache is is an equal quantity of double cream and chocolate heated together, it's easy to increase the volume of icing at your disposal.

I most often use, in cooking (and fall upon for eating), the most fabulous chocolate buttons made by a company called Montgomery Moore: the chocolate itself is incredibly good, and because it's already in buttons you don't have to chop it to make it easy to melt.

200g dark chocolate, with a minimum of 70% cocoa solids, chopped, or use chocolate buttons (see above)

200ml double cream

Put both ingredients in a saucepan and, over low heat, cook till the chocolate's melted. Whisk together with a Magiwhisk (for ease and preference), watching the mixture become thick and glossy. Spoon and smooth over your waiting cupcakes. After a couple of minutes' standing, decorate in whatever way you want.

BAGNA CAUDA

All good parties involve a lot of standing around gossiping and picking, and this is the food you want tableside to be picked from. I am loathe to say the word 'dip', but this is in effect what *bagna cauda* is, a ravishing Piedmontese velvety gunge of olive oil, garlic, anchovies and melted butter into which are speared raw florets of tight-budded ivory cauliflower, tightly furled chicory leaves, slices of courgette, fennel, chicory and red or (for aesthetic preference) yellow peppers and any other crudités that you want to provide.

Ideally, you want to keep the sauce warm, and for this you need either the traditional terracotta bowl that sits over a spirit burner or – oh joy of joys – a fondue bowl that can be placed over its candle-fitted stand to achieve the same purpose.

150ml extra-virgin olive oil
4–5 cloves of garlic, peeled and
  Microplaned
12 anchovies preserved in olive oil,
  drained and chopped

75–100g unsalted butter, cut into chunks

for dipping:
a variety of raw vegetables, including
  fennel, cauliflower, chicory, sweet
  peppers and courgettes

Put the oil in a pan with the garlic and anchovies and cook over a low heat, stirring, until you have a melted, muddy mess. Everything should begin to meld together. Whisk in 75g of butter, and as soon as it has melted, remove from the heat and give a few more beats of your whisk so that everything is creamy and amalgamated. Taste, and if you feel you want this dipping sauce – which is meant to be pungent but not acrid – a little more mellow, whisk in the remaining 25g of butter. Pour into a dish that, ideally, fits over a flame so that it does not get cold at the table.

Dip in the crudités and eat.

THE UNION SQUARE CAFE'S BAR NUTS

More picking food, and ludicrously easy to make. You might think that nuts, untampered with, are perfect picking food as they are, and up to a point you'd be right. But try these, modestly adapted from the recipe for the spiced nuts served at the Union Square Café in New York and you'll truly know what perfection is.

500g assorted unsalted nuts, including
   peeled peanuts, cashews, Brazil nuts,
   hazelnuts, walnuts, pecans and whole
   unpeeled almonds
2 tablespoons coarsely chopped fresh
   rosemary (from two 8cm sprigs)

1/2 teaspoon cayenne pepper
2 teaspoons dark muscovado sugar
2 teaspoons Maldon salt
1 tablespoon unsalted butter, melted

Preheat the oven to 180°C/gas mark 4.

Toss the nuts in a large bowl to combine and spread them out on a baking sheet. Toast in the oven till they become light golden-brown, about 10 minutes.

In a large bowl, combine the rosemary, cayenne, muscovado sugar, salt and melted butter.

Thoroughly toss the toasted nuts in the spiced butter and serve warm. And once you eat these, you will never want to stop.

HALLOUMI WITH CHILLI

I love grilled or fried halloumi, that squeaky, salty, polystyrene-textured cheese. Not a very seductive way of describing it maybe, but that, indeed, is what it's like. You should have no difficulty finding it in the supermarket, and this is a doddle to make. You don't need to do it at the very last minute, but don't fry the halloumi so far in advance that it's totally cooled by the time it comes to the table. And if you prefer, by all means grill it. And again, this is the sort of food that you can sit on the table for people idly to eat as they stand around, drink in hand. It looks beautiful, too, which is always an aid to proceedings.

2 tablespoons chopped, de-seeded fresh red chilli (about 2 medium chillies)
60ml (2 tablespoons) extra-virgin olive oil

2 x 250g packets of halloumi, sliced medium-thin (i.e., just under half a centimetre)
juice of ¼ lemon

Mix the chopped chilli and olive oil in a small bowl or cup and leave the flavours to deepen while you cook the cheese. I use a non-stick frying pan for this, without any oil, and just give the cheese slices about 2 minutes a side until they're golden-brown in parts. When all the slices of halloumi are cooked, transfer them to a couple of small plates. Give the chilli oil a stir, spoon it over the cheese, then give a spritz of lemon. That's all there is to it.

Makes about 30.

SPATCHCOCKED BIRDS

For that point in the evening when people need to hunker down to some serious eating, you do need to provide something a little more substantial than plates for picking from. This is what I roll out during a summer evening's barbecuing. You can stick with just chicken if you want, but I've suggested poussins and quail as well, just because I like anything that produces that welcoming sense of the groaning board – and plus, it gives me the opportunity to suggest more than one marinade.

The marinades themselves are to be regarded as the loosest blueprints. Use the flavourings you like, remembering that you need oil of some sort to prevent the meat from drying out and an acid – vinegar, citrus fruit – to tenderise it. The spatchcocked birds don't need to be cooked on the barbecue; an oven preheated to 220 or 240°C, gas mark 7 or 8, will do just fine. And because the birds are spatchcocked – that's to say, cut on one side and opened out like a book – they need much less cooking than surgically uninterfered with poultry, which can be useful if you've got time in advance for the spatchcocking and marinading and not much time on the night for actual cooking.

Any good butcher will spatchcock the birds for you, or you could ask the butchery section at the supermarket to do it, but it's easy enough for you to manage yourself at home. Just get a pair of poultry shears or tough scissors (I use a pair sold by someone on one of those door-to-door yellow-duster trails made for cutting through tins and tough stuff) and lay the bird, breast-side down, on a surface and cut all along one side of the backbone. Then cut along the other side and – hey presto – the backbone can be removed. You then turn the bird the other way up and press down as you open it out. You have in front of you a spatchcocked bird, ready for its marinade.

1 spatchcocked chicken, marinated in:
juice of 1 lemon
2 tablespoons black peppercorns, lightly
  crushed in pestle and mortar
100ml olive oil (not extra-virgin)
2 cloves of garlic, peeled and bruised

to sprinkle over:
Maldon salt
handful of fresh parsley, chopped

2 spatchcocked poussins, marinated in:
juice of 2 limes
2 tablespoons coriander seeds
100ml groundnut or vegetable oil
good grinding of black pepper

to sprinkle over:
Maldon salt
bunch of fresh coriander, chopped

4 spatchcocked quails, marinated in:
1 bunch of spring onions, sliced finely
100ml vegetable oil
dash of toasted sesame oil
2cm chunk fresh ginger, unpeeled and
  chopped roughly
1 tablespoon rice vinegar
1 tablespoon soy sauce

to sprinkle over:
Maldon salt
bunch of fresh coriander, chopped

Sit the birds in their marinade in a dish into which they fit snugly, cover with clingfilm and leave in the fridge, preferably overnight or for 24 hours, though even a couple of hours would have an effect.

When the barbecue is good and hot, lift the birds out of their marinade and cook on the barbie until the flesh has lost all raw pinkness but is still tender within and the skin is crisp and burnished and blistered. It's hard to be precise about times, since barbecues differ even more than ovens do, but on my barbecue – a gas-fired Outdoor Chef, which I love to distraction and, since it has a lid, I use even in the winter rain – the chicken takes about 35 minutes, the poussins 15 and the quail about 7.

Along with Maldon salt, sprinkle freshly chopped parsley over the chicken and coriander over the poussins and quail, or use whatever other herb seems right for the marinades you've concocted.

NOTES

NOTES

CHAPTER FIVE

RAINY DAYS

So much emphasis these days is put on fast-assembly food and skin-of-your-teeth cooking – which is fine, good even, for every day, but if the point of cooking is the end product, its meaning has to lie in the process. And sometimes, on house-bound rainy weekends or when you need to savour a little domestic warmth, you want to inhabit your kitchen, not merely rush through it.

PASTA WITH MEATBALLS

This is definitely time consuming, but here I make no apology for that. And there is nothing like serving up a bowl of pasta with meatballs to make you feel like an Italian mamma out of a Hollywood film. I don't mean one of those redoubtable types in amorphous black: think Sophia Loren in the kitchen. It works for me.

The trick to these meatballs is to keep them small. Don't actually use a teaspoon, but use about a teaspoon's amount of mince to roll each ball. If there are children around, so much the better; they tend to like making these. But otherwise, they're easy enough, and the slow repetitiveness of the action can be rather calming.

for the meatballs:
250g minced pork
250g minced beef
1 egg
2 tablespoons freshly grated parmesan

1 garlic clove, minced
1 teaspoon dried oregano
3 tablespoons semolina or breadcrumbs
good grind of black pepper
1 teaspoon salt

Just put everything in a large bowl and then, using your hands, mix to combine before shaping into small balls. Place the meatballs on baking sheets or plates that you have lined with clingfilm, and put each in the fridge as you finish them.

for the tomato sauce:
1 onion
2 cloves garlic
1 teaspoon dried oregano
1 tablespoon unsalted butter

1 tablespoon olive oil (not extra-virgin)
700g bottle tomato passata
pinch of sugar
salt and pepper
100ml full-fat milk

Put the onion, garlic and oregano into the processor and blitz to a pulp. Heat the butter and oil in a deep, wide pan, then scrape the onion-garlic mix into it and cook over low to medium heat for about 10 minutes. Don't let the mixture catch, just let it become soft. Add the bottle of passata and then half-fill the empty bottle with cold water. Add this to the pan with the pinch of sugar and some salt and pepper, and cook for about 10 minutes. The tomato sauce will appear thin at this stage, but don't worry as it will thicken a little later. Stir in the milk, and then drop the meatballs in one by one. Don't stir the pan until the meatballs have turned from pink to brown as you don't want to break them up. Cook everything for about 20 minutes, with the lid only partially covering it. At the end of cooking time, check the seasoning, as you may want more salt and a grind or two more of pepper.

Makes enough to sauce generously the pasta below, serving 6.

PASTA

To go with these divine meatballs, I like tagliatelle. De Cecco, Spinosi or Cipriani brands are all very good, but making fresh pasta is an experience worth trying. No one's saying you *have* to make it, but once you try, you'll soon see that it's not difficult. I had a pasta machine for years before I was brave enough to use it; for some reason I thought it would be a performance. But I tried and it isn't, and I rather like the mood of peaceful concentration the activity ushers forth. And it's a great way of playing in the kitchen with children: they love turning the handle, which is actually a help, not often the case when the children are cooking with you.

Quantities are easy so long as you remember you need 1 egg per 100g of 00 flour (now available at most supermarkets), and that, on average, one 'egg' of pasta, as it were, feeds two generously.

400g Italian 00 flour   **4 eggs**
fat pinch of salt

Either put the flour (with the salt) in a bowl and crack the eggs into it, or make a mound of flour on a worktop and add the eggs to that. I don't bother to beat them before adding them to the flour, but if you prefer to, do. Just find the way that you prefer. All you do is mix the flour and eggs together, and then knead the mixture until it all comes together in a satiny mass. Kneading involves no more than pushing the mixture away from you with the heels of your hands and then bringing it back towards you. If you've got an electric mixer with a dough hook, then use that, though for some reason I don't find it makes the pasta cohere any sooner. And you don't get the relaxing satisfaction of making it by hand.

When the pasta is silky and smooth, form it into a ball, cover with a cloth and leave for 30 minutes to an hour. Then get out your pasta machine, read the instructions and away you go. Two tips first: cut each slice you want to feed through the pasta machine as you go, and put through the no.1 press quite a few times, folding the strip in half and pushing it through again after each time. When the pasta dough's been fed a few times through the no.1 slot, pass it through the remaining numbers on the gauge, before pushing it through the tagliatelle-cutters. And I find that the pasta strips cut into tagliatelle better if you leave them hanging over the table or wherever to dry a little first (10 minutes is enough).

When you cook the pasta, make sure you've got plenty of boiling, salted water and start tasting immediately the water comes back to the boil after you've put the pasta in. Use about a third of the meatballs in their sauce to toss the cooked, drained pasta in and then pour the rest of them over the scantly sauced ribbons in the bowl. This is ambrosia: food to get you through the winter happily.

Serves 4–6.

SOFT AND SHARP INVOLTINI

I often make a southern-Italian dish of involtini: aubergines, sliced thinly, griddled and cooled, and then wrapped around a mixture of basil, pine nuts, breadcrumbs, garlic, provolone and parmesan, bound with egg, then baked in tomato sauce dotted with mozzarella. It's fiddly, but not difficult, and perfect for those times when you have the desire for a bit of slow pottering about in the kitchen. It also happens, as does this version, to be an incredibly useful standby for vile meat eaters like me who want to have something for vegetarians at a dinner party or whatever.

I've still called this involtini, although in truth there is nothing Italian about its component parts. The flavours are more Greek in nature: sharp feta, which perfectly off-sets the soft sweetness of the aubergines; and oregano, which is, dried and aromatic, *the* herb of the islands. It also occurred to me that using a dried herb made this a useful, year-round regular. In fact, it was my vegetarian option at my Christmas lunch last year.

I tend to do this in stages: the tomato sauce and griddled aubergines one day; the stuffing, wrapping and baking the next. And I love it at room temperature the next day, too.

for the sauce:
1 onion
1 clove garlic
half a teaspoon dried oregano
2 tablespoons olive oil
3 x 400g tins chopped tomatoes
2 teaspoons sugar
salt and pepper to taste
2 tablespoons extra-virgin olive oil
4 aubergines
olive oil for painting the aubergines
   (have plenty on hand)
ovenproof dish, approx. 30 x 21cm

for the stuffing:
100g bulgar wheat
1 teaspoon dried oregano
350ml boiling water
50g pistachios, roughly chopped
200g feta, crumbled
1 clove garlic, minced
1 fat or 2 thin spring onions, finely sliced
2 tablespoons capers (drained of
   vinegar)
1 egg
a pinch of cinnamon

for the top:
75g feta, crumbled
drizzle of olive oil
fat pinch of dried oregano

Peel and roughly chop the onion and press on the garlic with the flat of a knife to loosen the skin. Remove it and then sling onion, garlic and dried oregano into a food processor and blitz to a pulp. Cook in a deep, generous-sized pan (with a lid) in the 2 tablespoons of olive oil, over a medium to low heat, until softened – about 7 minutes. Add the tomatoes and the sugar, stir well, cover and turn down the heat, and let cook for about 20 minutes, checking often to see that the sauce is not bubbling too vociferously (and therefore sticking or drying out, or indeed both). Taste for seasoning, add salt and pepper or maybe a pinch more sugar if you feel it needs it, then stir again, add the extra-virgin olive oil, and take off the heat but keep the cover on. Leave till you need it.

Cut the aubergines in thinnish slices lengthways and chuck away the two skin-covered edges: you need to be able to roll the aubergine lengths up later and so you need the full extent. It may sound wasteful, but I'm happy if I get 4–5 good slices per aubergine. Put some oil into a bowl and using a pastry brush, paint each slice generously with the oil. Then cook them on a hot griddle until bronzed, striped without and tender within. Or you can dispense with all the painting procedure and just fry the aubergine slices in a pan filled to about half a centimetre's depth of olive oil. In either case, remove the cooked slices to sheets of kitchen towel to absorb excess oil. Cook all the aubergine slices this way and then, when cool, you can either begin the stuffing and rolling, or set them aside until you want to. If I'm doing this in advance, I line a dish with baking parchment, arrange a layer of aubergine slices on top, then cover with baking parchment, then another layer of aubergines and so on, until I've packed them all away. Cover with a layer of baking parchment and leave till needed.

I tend to stuff the aubergines shortly before cooking them. Measure the bulgar wheat into a bowl, add the dried oregano, pour over the water and cover with a plate. Leave to steep for 30 minutes. Meanwhile, preheat the oven to 190°C/gas mark 5, and oil your ovenproof dish lightly.

When the bulgar wheat has had its time, pour it into a large sieve and press down to remove excess water. Leave for a few minutes till it's cooled a little and then decant to a large bowl. Add about two-thirds of the chopped pistachios (you just need to leave some for sprinkling when serving), the crumbled feta, minced garlic, spring onions and capers. Stir to mix, but don't be too heavy-handed about it: a few goes with a fork should be enough to combine everything. Beat the egg with the cinnamon and fork this in, too. I find it easier after that's done just to weigh in with my hands, squeezing everything together so you've got a cohesive, nubbly stuffing in front of you.

Get out the aubergines and, one by one, place them in front of you, stalk end at the top, bulbous bottom nearest you. Add a dollop of stuffing at the bottom, roll up lengthways away from you and put each fat little bundle in the oiled dish as you go. When they're all sitting there snuggly, pour over the tomato sauce, scatter over the 75g of crumbled feta, drizzle with oil, sprinkle over a little dried oregano and cook for 30 minutes. Remove from the oven and let stand at least 15 minutes before serving: this shouldn't be piping hot. Scatter with the remaining pistachios before bringing it to the table.

Serves 4 as a main course.

PASTA E FAGIOLI

This is that life-saving, thick, pasta-and-bean meal of a soup as sung about by Dean Martin in 'That's Amore'. It's just the thing you want to eat when the rain's battering against the window panes and just what you need to cook to make you feel that you're safe and warm, happy and occupied within.

I have to say, it's the first time I've included a popsock among any list of ingredients. By all means bundle the rosemary and onion into a muslin cloth if it makes you feel more satisfactorily homespun, but I am just not one of those efficiently traditional domestic types that keeps cheesecloths and muslins on hand.

500g borlotti beans
5 cloves of garlic, whole, plus 1,
**   Microplaned or grated**
1 popsock
2 leafy sprigs of rosemary
1 onion, peeled and quartered
salt to taste

1 tablespoon tomato concentrate
3 tablespoons olive oil
sprig of rosemary, about 6cm, needles
**   finely chopped**
200g ditalini or other small pasta tubes
extra-virgin olive oil, to serve

Put the borlotti beans in a large bowl, cover with cold water and let the beans soak overnight or for at least 6 hours.

Drain the beans and tip them into a large saucepan. Using the flat side of a large knife, press down on the whole garlic cloves so that their papery skins tear and begin to come away. Peel them and chuck the bruised cloves on top of the beans. Now take your popsock and in it pop, appropriately enough, the sprigs of rosemary and cut-up onion. This will stop the needles (which turn bitter on boiling) from infiltrating the soup (very irritating between the teeth, too) but allow their resiny fragrance to seep through. I also find it better not to have slimy onion skins all over the place later. Cover everything generously with cold water, clamp on a lid and bring to the boil. Once it's started boiling, turn the heat down and simmer for an hour. Check the beans to see how cooked they are and, only when they're tender, add salt to taste.

Chuck out the corpsed popsock and its contents. Remove a mugful of beans – or more if you want a very thick soup – and tip into a blender (my preference) or processor, along with a tablespoonful of tomato concentrate and 250ml of the bean-cooking liquid and liquidise.

Now, add the 3 tablespoons of oil to a small saucepan and grate (I always use my fine Microplane for this) or squeeze in the sixth clove of garlic. Cook over a low to medium heat until soft but not coloured and then stir in the finely chopped rosemary. Cook for another scant minute, add the liquidised soup and cook for a minute or so, then tip into the large pan of beans. Bring back to the boil and add the ditalini, cooking them according to packet instructions. Drizzle with extra-virgin olive oil and serve.

Serves 8.

CHOCOLATE CLOUD CAKE

On days when I want the warmth of the hearth rather than the hurly burly of the city streets I stay in and read cookery books, and this recipe comes from just the sort of book that gives most succour, *Classic Home Desserts* by Richard Sax. The cake itself (which was the pudding I made for last New Year's Eve dinner) is as richly and rewardingly sustaining: a melting, dark, flourless, chocolate base, the sort that sinks damply on cooling; the fallen centre then cloudily filled with softly whipped cream and sprinkled with cocoa powder. As Richard Sax says, 'intensity, then relief, in each bite'.

250g dark chocolate, minimum 70%
  cocoa solids
125g unsalted butter, softened
6 eggs: 2 whole, 4 separated
175g caster sugar
2 tablespoons Cointreau (optional)
grated zest of 1 orange (optional)
23cm springform cake tin

for the cream topping:
500ml double cream
1 teaspoon vanilla extract
1 tablespoon Cointreau (optional)
½ teaspoon unsweetened cocoa
  powder for sprinkling

Preheat the oven to 180°C/gas mark 4.

Line the bottom of the cake tin with baking parchment.

Melt the chocolate either in a double boiler or a microwave, and then let the butter melt in the warm chocolate.

Beat the 2 whole eggs and 4 egg yolks with 75g of the caster sugar, then gently add the chocolate mixture, the Cointreau and orange zest.

In another bowl, whisk the 4 egg whites until foamy, then gradually add the 100g of sugar and whisk until the whites are holding their shape but not too stiff. Lighten the chocolate mixture with a dollop of egg whites, and then fold in the rest of the whites. Pour into the prepared tin and bake for 35–40 minutes or until the cake is risen and cracked and the centre is no longer wobbly. Cool the cake in its tin on a wire rack; the middle will sink as it cools.

When you are ready to eat, place the still tin-bound cake on a cake stand or plate for serving and carefully remove the cake from its tin. Don't worry about cracks or rough edges: it's the crater look we're going for here. Whip the cream until it's soft and then add the vanilla and Cointreau and continue whisking until the cream is firm but not stiff. Fill the crater of the cake with the whipped cream, easing it out gently towards the edges of the cake, and dust the top lightly with cocoa powder pushed through a tea-strainer.

Serves 8–12.

You can make this into an Easter Nest Cake by folding 200g melted chocolate into the cream topping and dotting with the sugar-coated eggs instead of the cocoa. Leave the Cointreau out of both the cake and cream.

RASPBERRY AND LEMONGRASS TRIFLE

Trifle is the perfect thing to cook when you've got protracted time to busy yourself quietly in the kitchen. No one stage takes long, but the whole needs to be lingered over. And if it sounds odd to suggest steeping the sponges in a syrup flavoured with lemongrass, I should say that I first had the idea when making a syrup with lemon balm for some jelly. If you've got a garden, this is easy to come by, but if you haven't there is no way you can buy it. I tried, then, substituting lemongrass, weight for weight, and it worked beautifully. By the same token, if you have got verbena in the garden then do use that here. But since there isn't a supermarket around that doesn't major in lemongrass – and indeed it's far more familiar to us than the indigenous lemon balm – this recipe, which first found shape in an *Observer* article on cooking traditional British foods with new 'fusion' ingredients, is actually a good reminder that you can plunder the past without scorning the present.

600ml water
400g caster sugar
50g lemongrass, 3–4 sticks, cut in half
   lengthways
300g raspberries
16 trifle sponges

3–4 tablespoons vodka
600ml single cream
8 egg yolks
500ml double cream
medium glass bowl

Make a syrup with the water and 325g of the caster sugar by bringing them to the boil in a saucepan and boiling for 5 minutes. Take the pan off the heat, add the lemongrass and let it infuse for about half an hour.

Strain the syrup into a measuring jug, keeping the saucepan with the lemongrass to one side. Take out about 150–200ml of the syrup and put it into a pan with the raspberries. Bring it to a rolling boil and let it thicken slightly, mashing the fruit to make a jam-like consistency. Let it cool a little and then dunk the trifle sponges in the raspberry mixture and arrange them in the bottom of your bowl. Add the vodka and about 100ml of the lemongrass syrup depending on how much your sponges absorb, and reserve the rest.

Meanwhile, to make the custard, heat the single cream in the syrup pan with the lemongrass until it is nearly boiling, take it off the heat and let it infuse for about 15 minutes. Whisk the yolks and the rest of the sugar together and pour the cream into the same bowl. Then whisk again and put the custard back on the heat in the cleaned-out pan. Stir until the custard thickens and then pour it over the trifle sponges. Let it cool.

Whip the double cream until thick but not stiff, and cover the custard layer. Use about 250ml of the remaining sugar syrup to make a caramel by heating it in a saucepan until it turns a golden-brown. Drizzle the caramelised sugar syrup over the layer of cream to decorate.

Serves 8–10.

RAINY-DAY BISCUITS

If you've got children, you'll know all about the problems of keeping them occupied when the weather's bad and outdoors uninviting – if only to you. Actually, I go further than that. I am singularly unathletic and rather dread extended bouts on the swings in the park even on sunny days. Cooking is thus, for me, the easiest childcare option. And even two-year-olds can be usefully entertained with a bit of dough and some biscuit cutters. Yes, the kitchen will be a mess, but the afternoon will be gone, and then there's just bath- and bed-time to be got through – then peace: a small price, then.

I wouldn't go so far as to say I collect biscuit cutters, but I ask anyone who's going abroad to buy any amusing form they find and seem to have acquired a stash of curious shapes. The ones that were used for the pictures below were from this disorganised jumble and seemed best suited to making biscuits to banish rainy-day blues.

175g soft unsalted butter	**1 teaspoon salt**
200g soft brown sugar	**biscuit cutters**
2 eggs	**2 non-stick baking sheets**
¼ teaspoon almond extract	
350g plain flour (plus more if needed)	*for the icing:*
50g ground almonds	**approx. 300g icing sugar**
1 teaspoon baking powder	**water to mix**

Preheat the oven to 180°C/gas mark 4.

Cream the butter and sugar together well until almost moussy, then beat in the eggs and almond extract.

In another bowl, combine the flour, ground almonds, baking powder and salt. Gradually add these dry ingredients to the butter and egg mixture and combine gently but surely. If you think the finished mixture is too sticky to be rolled out, add more flour, but do so sparingly as too much will make the dough tough.

Halve the dough, form into fat discs, wrap each in clingfilm and rest in the fridge for at least an hour.

Sprinkle a suitable surface with flour, place a disc of dough (not taking out the other half until you've finished with the first) on top of it and sprinkle a little more flour on top of that. Then roll it out to a thickness of about half a centimetre. This dough is such a dream to work that it makes this a rather pleasurable activity.

Cut into shapes, dipping the cutter into flour as you go, and place the cut-out biscuits a little apart on the baking sheets.

Bake for 8–12 minutes, by which time they will be lightly golden around the edges but otherwise still quite pale. Cool on a rack – they do firm up when they're cold – and continue with the rest of the dough.

It's hard to be accurate about the number of biscuits you'll get out of this mixture without knowing what cutters you'll be using, but in general I reckon on making 60 biscuits out of the above quantities.

As for the icing: who am I to interfere with the artist within you? All I would do is urge you to try and get hold of the colour pastes which come in little tubs (and can be bought from specialised cake shops and increasingly, though not with such an expansive range, in supermarkets) rather than use those little bottles of liquid food colouring. The choice of colours is better, for one thing, and they don't water down the icing when you add them.

NOTES

CHAPTER SIX

TRASHY

Enjoying food, enjoying eating, isn't about graduating with honours from the Good Taste university. I'm not interested in pleasing food snobs or purists, or in eating just one type of food. Yes, I want whatever I do eat to be good, but there is surely a place – and in my heart a very fond one – for a bit of kitsch in the kitchen.

HAM IN COCA-COLA

This recipe is from *How to Eat*, with some rejigging (just because it's not in my nature to leave completely alone), and I don't apologise for reproducing, or rather recasting, it because I simply cannot urge you to try this strongly enough. The first time I made it, it was, to be frank, really just out of amused interest. I'd heard, and read, about this culinary tradition from the deep South, but wasn't expecting it, in all honesty, to be good. The truth is it's magnificent, and makes converts of anyone who eats it. But, if you think about it, it's not surprising it should work: the sweet, spiky drink just infuses it with spirit of barbecue. I have to force myself to cook ham any other way now; though often I don't bother with the glaze but just leave it for longer in the bubbling Coke instead.

And the salty, sweet liquor it leaves behind in the pot after it's cooked makes an instant base for the most fabulous black bean soup.

But just one thing before we start: don't even consider using Diet Coke; it's full-fat or nothing.

2kg mild-cure gammon
1 onion, peeled and cut in half
2-litre bottle of Coca-Cola

for the glaze:
handful of cloves
1 heaped tablespoon black treacle
2 teaspoons English mustard powder
2 tablespoons demerara sugar

I find now that mild-cure gammon doesn't need soaking, but if you know that you're dealing with a salty piece, then put it in a pan covered with cold water, bring to the boil, then tip into a colander in the sink and start from here; otherwise, put the gammon in a pan, skin-side down if it fits like that, add the onion, then pour over the Coke. Bring to the boil, reduce to a good simmer, put the lid on, though not tightly, and cook for just under 2½ hours. If your joint is larger or smaller, work out timing by reckoning on an hour per kilo, remembering that it's going to get a quick blast in the oven later. But do take into account that if the gammon's been in the fridge right up to the moment you cook it, you will have to give it a good 15 minutes or so extra so that the interior is properly cooked.

Meanwhile, preheat the oven to 240°C/gas mark 9.

When the ham's had its time (and ham it is, now it's cooked, though it's true Americans call it ham from its uncooked state) take it out of the pan (but do NOT throw away the cooking liquid) and let cool a little for ease of handling. (Indeed, you can let it cool completely then finish off the cooking at some later stage if you want.) Then remove the skin, leaving a thin layer of fat. Score the fat with a sharp knife to make fairly large diamond shapes, and stud each diamond with a clove. Then carefully spread the treacle over the bark-budded skin, taking care not to dislodge the cloves. Gently pat the mustard and sugar onto the sticky fat. Cook in a foil-lined roasting tin for approximately 10 minutes or until the glaze is burnished and bubbly.

Should you want to do the braising stage in advance and then let the ham cool, clove and glaze it and give it 30–40 minutes, from room temperature, at 180°C/gas mark 4, turning up the heat towards the end if you think it needs it.

This is seriously fabulous with anything, but the eggily golden sweetcorn pudding that follows is perfect: ham and eggs Southern style.

Serves 8.

SWEETCORN PUDDING

This isn't pudding as in dessert, but as in rich, heavy, airless soufflé. I suppose there's nothing to stop you separating the eggs, whisking the whites and turning this into a lighter, frothier affair, but there is most definitely no call. This is easy to make, toothsome and comforting to eat, and I have Gabbie de Jersey to thank for it.

There's something particularly gratifying in specifying a can of cream-style sweetcorn in a recipe, but then I have a great sentimental affection for it. When I was about twelve, it was my idea of gastronomic heaven. And needless to say, children love this: thrown together, in smaller quantities to be sure, and paired with some slices of shop-bought ham, it makes for a simple, stress-free tea, one that's likely to be eaten, not pushed whiningly to the side of the plate.

5 eggs
510g can sweetcorn, drained
418g can creamed sweetcorn
300ml full-fat milk

300ml double cream
60g plain flour
½ teaspoon baking powder
½ teaspoon salt

Preheat the oven to 190°C/gas mark 5 and butter an ovenproof dish – and I use my old, scuffed Pyrex one which measures 33 x 25cm.

Whisk the eggs in a large bowl, and then add, beating unenergetically, all the other ingredients. Pour into the buttered dish and cook for about an hour, by which time it should have set within and puffed up slightly on the top.

Serves 8.

SOUTH-BEACH BLACK BEAN SOUP

This soup bears the name of one in *How to Eat*, but is very different in composition. There are fewer ingredients in it and fewer demands on the cook who makes it. But how could I lose such a title – in this chapter of all places?

The point about this is that it provides a way of using up the sweet, dark liquor that the Coke-cooked ham has left behind. I know I'm extravagant but, as I'm so fond of intoning, I'm never wasteful, and this is a rewarding way of satisfying my need to use up every last thing in the kitchen. It's not as if you need to make the soup right away; by all means freeze the stock for future soups if you want. In terms of flavour, I dare say it could be used for a variety of soups, but there is an aesthetic factor to be considered – which isn't the same thing as being queeny about presentation. The point about black beans is that they're black: what do they care about the colour of the stock they're simmered in? If anything, the sludgy darkness of this liquid enhances their muddy glory.

I never soak black beans: just make sure that when you cook them they get their 10 toxin-destroying minutes of vociferous boiling and you're away.

500g black beans	***to serve:***
Coca-Cola ham stock from recipe above	**sour cream**
juice of ½ lime	**fresh coriander, chopped**
1 teaspoon ground cumin	**lime wedges**
1 teaspoon ground coriander	

Cook the black beans in the Coca-Cola ham stock until they're tender. Remove about 3 ladles of the soup to a blender, add the lime juice and ground spices, blitz to a muddy purée and stir this back into the pan of soup. And that's it.

Swirl some sour cream, as you please, into the bowls of soup as you ladle them out and sprinkle with freshly chopped coriander. Plonk the lime wedges onto the table and let people squeeze the sharp juice into this dense, sweet soup as they eat.

Serves 8.

CORNBREAD-ON-THE-COB

The golden sweetness of cornbread goes perfectly with the dark intensity of the black bean soup. Now, you can make cornbread in loaf, square or muffin tins, but I love the cornbread that comes in cornsticks – made by cooking the mixture in cast-iron moulds that resemble folk art themselves, to give the nubbly form of corn-on-the-cob. There's just something about making food in funny shapes, however soberly compelling the taste, that just has 'trashy' all over it, and is very gratifying too sometimes. You can buy these sorts of moulds, over here now, though not usually in cast iron, but I've got some that a friend devotedly schlepped over for me all the way from the Broadway Panhandler in New York (a shop with stock as good as its name) which I understandably cherish.

Get some if you can, especially if you've got children, to whom, though not exclusively, they appeal. And eat these golden miniature maize breads with stews, the black bean soup above, with fried eggs and bacon, or just as they are, for breakfast.

vegetable shortening for greasing cornsticks, or butter for tins
175g fine cornmeal (or polenta: same difference really)
125g plain flour
45g caster sugar

fat pinch of salt
1 tablespoon baking powder
250ml full-fat milk
1 egg
45g unsalted butter, melted and cooled

Preheat the oven to 200°C/gas mark 6 then grease the cornstick moulds with melted vegetable shortening. Those sadly lacking in the cornstick-mould department should grease a square 20cm tin (5cm deep) or 12-bun muffin tin with butter (if you're not using paper cases).

Mix the cornmeal, flour, sugar, salt and baking powder in a large bowl. In a measuring jug beat together the milk, egg and cooled, melted butter. Then pour the wet ingredients into the dry, stirring with a wooden spoon until just combined. Don't worry in the slightest about the odd lump. Pour into the greased moulds and bake for 12–15 minutes for the cornsticks or 20–25 minutes for the square or muffin tins. When ready, the cornbread should be just pulling away from the sides.

Cut the square, if using, into smaller, chunky squares or tip out the cornsticks or muffins and eat warm. And these cornsticks, swabbed with butter as if you really were eating corn-on-the-cob, are God's way of telling you that greed really is good.

Makes 18 cornsticks, 12 muffins or 9 x 7cm squares of cornbread.

WATERMELON DAIQUIRI

The trashy cook should not be stoveside too long without a drink in hand. And preferably this drink. You don't have to go overboard with the postmodern, anxiously ironic bit: this is ambrosia for even the good-taste gods.

But if on the other hand you're concerned that commendation might detract from its vulgar charm, just make it and drink it, wearing mules to match.

The watermelon doesn't come frozen, by the way, engaging thought though that is: just buy it, slice it, chunk it, stuff it into suitable bags and stash them vibrantly in the freezer.

100ml (or to taste) Bacardi
juice of 1 good-sized lime
1 heaped tablespoon icing sugar

approx. 10 x 5cm cubes of frozen watermelon

Put all the above ingredients in a blender and blitz to a pinkly foamy purée. Pour into two waiting marguerita glasses – and tip back, bangles jangling.

SOUTHERN-STYLE CHICKEN

There's something about frying, especially in vegetable shortening and in such Rosanne-like quantities, that is so refreshingly unchic. But I assure you there's no element of let's-go-slumming smuggery about the inclusion of this recipe here, for all the glee I take in the gorgeously garish wrapper in which my vegetable fat of choice comes. This is exceptionally good, a taste sensation and textural heaven; bite into it and savour a fine-ly balanced contrast – tender, poached meat within, crisp coating seared onto it – that the great names of the old Nouvelle Cuisine could only dream of.

Southern cooks use buttermilk for steeping, and fry their soak-softened meat from raw. I use ordinary milk, and poach the chicken in it before frying. Whether this makes it authentically Southern-fried chicken I wouldn't like to say, but regard this as *homage* rather than imitation.

2 chicken drumsticks, skin on
2 chicken thigh portions, skin on,
  bone in
750ml–1 litre full-fat milk (see below)
1 tablespoon plus 1 teaspoon salt

125g plain flour
1 teaspoon cayenne pepper
1 egg, beaten
500g solid vegetable fat for frying

Put the chicken pieces in a dish into which they fit snugly. Pour over the milk to cover and sprinkle over the tablespoon of salt. Dibble with your fingers to mix in. Cover with clingfilm and leave in the fridge for a few hours or overnight. (You don't absolutely have to do this, but it will help tenderise the meat.)

Tip the contents of the dish into a pan with a lid and bring to the boil, turning it down to simmer until the chicken pieces are entirely cooked through. The pan will look like a horrible, clumpy, curdy mess but don't be put off – it makes the chicken taste wonderful later, which is what matters. Also it's hard to fry chicken really well (or I find it so) from raw, as the skin tends to burn before the meat's cooked at the bone. This is simply my way of resolving this.

Remove the chicken pieces to a rack and let cool; they don't need to be cold, but you don't want them still steamy. Put the flour, cayenne and teaspoon of salt into a plastic bag, shake all the pieces of chicken in it one by one, then dip them into the egg, then into the flour again.

Leave to dry on the rack for about 15 minutes. Heat the great white slab of vegetable fat in a frying pan until it's nearly at smoking point. Don't worry about using so much: the more fat and the hotter it is, the less the food you're cooking absorbs. So, untroubled, lower in the chicken pieces and cook for a minute or so each side – just long enough for the skin to crisp and turn a rich golden-brown.

Eat hot, straight from the pan, with crisps and a green salad – or, believe it or not, cold. These gold-and-bronzed beauties make killer picnic food.

Serves 2–4.

ELVIS PRESLEY'S FRIED PEANUT-BUTTER AND BANANA SANDWICH

Let's not mess around: you want trashy, I'll give you trashy – I'll give you the King. This recipe, for want of a better word, comes from a rhinestone gem of a cookbook, *Are You Hungry Tonight?*, a collection of his favourite foodstuffs bought on a visit to Graceland many years back, prized ever since and a delight from cover to cover. Even my most recent addition to a library already bursting with bad-taste titles, *Liberace Cooks!*, can't lose him his crown.

You'd think, wouldn't you, that smearing a couple of slabs of white bread with peanut butter and mashed banana, sandwiching the lot bulgingly together and then frying it in butter, would be at best revolting. But that's where you'd be wrong. I have no particular fondness for peanut butter, or bananas for that matter, and a downright shuddering aversion to eating them cooked, but what a genius that man was. This sandwich is a wondrous thing, gloriously exemplifying what cooking is all about: the whole is so much intriguingly, confoundingly more than the sum of its parts. It really works. I wouldn't turn one down now at any time, although, true to form, there is a certain kamikaze calorie-intake involved not always to be calmly countenanced – but for a hangover, to combat seediness and restore the fragmenting self, it's particular perfection: it doesn't merely sustain, it resuscitates.

Believe it or not, the quantities below appear in edited, attenuated form. I honour the King but I can't be him.

1 small ripe banana
2 slices white bread

2 scant tablespoons smooth peanut butter (don't use extra-smooth)
2 tablespoons butter

Mash or slice the banana.

Lightly toast the bread, and then spread the peanut butter on one piece and the banana on the other. Sandwich together then fry in the butter, turning once, until each side is golden-brown. Remove to a plate, cut the sandwich carefully in half on the diagonal and eat.

Serves 1.

DEEP-FRIED BOUNTIES WITH PINEAPPLE

Or Glasgow meets the Caribbean. Francis MacNeil, the lighting assistant on the series, told me about the joys of deep-fried Bounty (far in excess, I should say, of the more familiar regional dish of deep-fried Mars Bar) and since I had people coming for dinner at the end of that week, I just had to try it. I should say that I offered it as a perfectly serious pudding – more or less – after a starter of tuna with ginger, soy and rice vinegar, a take on the salmon recipe on p178 and the Thai seafood curry on p66: it was a triumph.

The pineapple cuts across the sticky sweetness of the fritters and turns it into a pudding rather than a funny turn. Besides, the combination of coconut and pineapple is a time-honoured one. You might consider putting a bottle of good rum on the table for people to drink alongside, too.

As for the batter: I find the combination of self-raising flour and fizzy water produces the lightest effect possible.

And since then, I have been inspired to move on to deep fried Cadbury's Creme Eggs (a must for Easter) and deep-fried Dime Bars. There's no stopping me now...

approx. 2 litres sunflower or other oil for deep frying

1 ripe pineapple

150g self-raising flour

200-225ml fizzy water

8 x fun-sized Bounty bars

Heat the oil in a deep-fat fryer to maximum heat.

Cut the top and bottom off the pineapple, and then quarter it vertically. Trim the woody core off each segment, and then lie it skin-side down, and slice the flesh in half lengthways, stopping when you feel the skin. Then cut it across into slices and run the knife between the flesh of the fruit and the outer husk. The pineapple pieces should then come away easily. Squeeze the outer skin of the pineapple over the cut fruit to get every last bit of juice.

Measure the flour into a bowl, and whisk in 175ml of the fizzy water to make the batter, adding the rest of the water if the consistency is still too thick: you want this just thick enough to adhere easily. The best way to check is to turn a Bounty in it: if the batter sticks well enough, it's fine. I just use my fingers for this, but tongs work well too.

Plunge the batter-blanketed Bounties in the hot oil and fry for about 3 minutes until the batter's puffed and golden. Remove to pieces of kitchen towel to absorb excess grease, then pile up on a plate to sit on the table alongside the cut-up pineapple.

CHOCOLATE-LIME CHEESECAKE

Perhaps it is eccentric to wait for the last recipe in the chapter before pausing to explain what it is that makes any food trashy, as far as my purposes here are concerned, but nothing exemplifies it better than this cheesecake. Right then: you should know I start from the premise – and this is resolutely the case with all the recipes here – that, all campness aside, it has to be good – better than good: it can taste surprisingly elegant or prejudice-challengingly seductive, but the one thing it mustn't taste like is a joke.

If that's understood, we can move on. Trashy food, in its platonic ideal, should contain at least one brand-name product. Here we have the Philadelphia cream cheese leading. Next, it should use a low-rent ingredient, one that gastro-snobs would never normally even consider keeping in the house: may I introduce you to Maryland cookies? (Yes, I like them too, but we're talking culinary status-queens here, the pose of the label-conscious purist.) Finally, in its loftiest incarnation, it should seek to evoke some food or food-related substance that is industrially produced, not naturally occurring. Here, my inspiration for the cheesecake (itself widely considered a declassé foodstuff, certainly one devalued by inferior evocations) was a sweet – those chocolate limes I ate in my childhood.

That the base is rich and dark and perfectly counters the light, tender cream-cheese custard above it, itself kept all the more delicately smooth by being baked in a water bath (and this is easy: don't let a bit of wrapping in foil and boiling a kettle put you off before you start) and made intensely, fragrantly sharp by having the juice of four uncompromisingly sour limes squeezed into it, takes us back to the beginning. Trashy is a state of mind, a game of mood: the food itself deserves, *demands*, to be served and eaten – unsmirkingly, unapologetically and with voluptuous and exquisite pleasure.

200g Double Choc Maryland cookies (in the purple packet)	4 whole eggs
75g unsalted butter	2 yolks
750g Philadelphia cream cheese	juice of 4 limes
200g caster sugar	20–21cm springform cake tin
	kitchen foil

Place a large overlapping piece of foil over the bottom of the springform tin, and then insert the pan ring over it. Fold the foil up around the sides of the tin and place the whole thing on a second piece of foil, also folding it and pressing it securely up around the tin so that you have a water-tight covering. Actually, I sometimes find some water dribbles out from this supposedly secure casing on unwrapping, but it doesn't seem – as long as you unwrap the outer later straightaway – to cause any sogginess.

Process the biscuits until they are like crumbs, then add the butter and pulse again. Line the bottom of the springform tin, pressing the biscuits in with your hands or the back of a spoon. Put the tin in the fridge to set, and preheat the oven to 180°C/gas mark 4.

Beat the cream cheese gently until it's smooth, and then add the sugar. Beat in the eggs and egg yolks, then finally the lime juice. Put a full kettle on.

Pour the cream cheese filling onto the chilled biscuit base, place the tin in a roasting tray and pour hot water from the recently boiled kettle around the foil-wrapped cheesecake to come about halfway up the sides of the springform; don't overfill as you'll only spill it on the way to the oven. Transfer it as steadily as you can to the oven and cook for 1 hour or so, checking after 50 minutes. It should feel set, but not rigidly so. You want to be able to detect, below the skin, the slightest, sexiest hint of quiver within.

Take the roasting tin out of the oven, then gingerly remove the springform from its water-filled tin, stand it on a rack, peel off the outer layer of foil, tear away the side bits of the first layer of foil and leave to cool. When the cheesecake's cooled down completely, place it in the fridge and leave it there till 20 minutes or so before you want to eat it.

Transfer to the plate you're going to serve it on (it will need to be one without a lip, or a cakestand) and unclip. The underneath bit of the first layer of foil, along with the base of the tin, are going to have to stay in place, unless you like living really dangerously. I don't mind a bit of risk in the kitchen, but fiddling about with something as desirably lacking in solidity as this dreamlike cheesecake is beyond even my clumsily impatient foolhardiness.

It makes life easier if, when you cut it, you heat the knife and cake slicer (and I find I need to use both, the one to cut, the other to lift up and ferry slice to waiting plate) under a very hot tap first.

Serves 8.

NOTES

_____

_____

_____

_____

_____

_____

_____

_____

_____

_____

_____

_____

_____

_____

_____

NOTES

CHAPTER SEVEN

LEGACY

The way I cook, more than what I cook, is so much a product of the way my mother cooked before me, and most of what I feel about food comes from my family. Every time I pick up a pan I am drawing on what I inherited – cooking is nothing if not about temperament and habit – but there are some special dishes which I either ate as a child, or which come from the family kitchen that have a special significance and which I want to keep alive and pass on.

ITALIAN SAUSAGES WITH LENTILS

My mother used English sausages mostly, and those flat, sludgy lentils (Puy lentils weren't so easily available then) but this is at its best made with highly flavoured Italian sausages (I love the ones tagged 'Genovese', deep with garlic and basil) and either French Puy lentils or the similar Italian ones from Umbria.

This isn't about fancifying a downhome dish: it's about doing what feels right and responding to what's available; in short, it's about cooking.

This incidentally, is what Italians serve traditionally on New Year's Day; the coin-shaped lentils symbolise the prosperity that is hoped for over the coming year, much as Jewish tradition uses honey richly for the Rosh Hashanah meal to represent the wish for a sweet and happy life for the year ahead.

3–4 tablespoons olive oil (not extra-virgin)
1 onion, finely chopped
sprinkling of salt
500g Puy lentils
1 fat clove garlic, squished with the side of a knife, and skin removed

8 Italian sausages
100ml red wine
50ml water
flat-leaf parsley for sprinkling

To cook the lentils, put 2–3 tablespoons of the oil into a good-sized saucepan (and one which has a lid that fits) on the heat and when it's warm add the chopped onion. Sprinkle with salt (which helps prevents it browning) and cook over a low to medium heat till soft (about 5 minutes). Add the lentils, stir well and then cover generously with cold water. Bring to the boil, then cover and let simmer gently for half an hour or so until cooked and most, if not all, the liquid's absorbed. I don't add salt at this stage since the sauce provided by the sausages later (and which will be poured over the lentils) will be pretty salty itself. So, wait and taste. And remember, you can of course cook the lentils in advance.

Anyway, when either the lentils are nearly ready or you're about to reheat them, put a heavy-based frying pan on the hob, cover with a film of oil and add the bruised garlic. Cook for a few minutes then add and brown the sausages. When the sausages are brown on both sides – which won't take more than 5 minutes or so – throw in the wine and water and let bubble up. Cover the pan, either with a lid or tin foil, and cook for about 15 minutes. Using a fork, mash the now-soft garlic into the sauce and taste for seasoning, adding a little more water if it's too strong.

Remove the lentils to a shallowish bowl or dish (I evacuate the sausages from their cooking pan, plonk the lentils in, then proceed) then cover with the sausages and their garlicky, winey gravy. Sprinkle over some flat-leaf parsley.

Serves 4.

SOFT-BOILED EGGS WITH ASPARAGUS SOLDIERS

No, we didn't eat this for breakfast when I was a child, so keep calm. It's just that I remember eating asparagus like this, dipped into oily-yolked soft-boiled eggs or pronged into the soft, bulging, yellow belly of a fried one (in which case, it becomes Asparagus Holstein). It's a good way of making the expensive bundles of early English asparagus go further and, besides, the richness of the flowing, viscous yolk provides the best and simplest sauce for the bud-tipped grass. Consider serving this as a starter; go further, too, if you like and provide plates of puce-pink salty-sweet prosciutto, the slices to be used as edible damask napkins with which to wrap and hold the juicy green stems.

1 bunch of asparagus	**Maldon salt**
4 eggs at room temperature	

Cut the woody ends off the asparagus, and cook it in a shallow saucepan of boiling water until it's tender but still has some bite – about 5 minutes. Then drain them and keep them warm while you cook the eggs.

In a saucepan, bring some water to the boil into which you have dropped a matchstick; according to my Aunt Frieda this stops the white from billowing out into the pan should the egg crack while cooking. Am I going to promise this works? Well, all families have their folklore.

Lower the eggs into the water and cook them at a steady boil for about 4 minutes. Take them out of the water and immediately slice the top off each one; the yolk should still be runny enough to dip the asparagus spears in.

Make sure there's salt on the table for sprinkling into the almost aggressive blandness of the egg and spear, as you eat, with the warm asparagus.

Serves 4.

WHITEBAIT

I'd almost forgotten about whitebait until I saw it in the fishmonger's recently, and – in honour of my new(ish) deep-fat fryer – bought it and took it home to cook. When I was a child, this was *the* restaurant starter; now it seems to have disappeared from the menu altogether. I didn't eat it then, but my father and sister, Thomasina, always ordered it, and it is partly in her memory, and with the wish that she was still here to eat it, that I present it to you now.

It is so unfamiliar now that some of you may need me to tell you what whitebait is, or are. Whitebait is just small fish, indeed the original 'small fry', and it's the size rather than the genus that's significant. Generally, it refers to very young herring or sprats, and these are deep-fried and eaten whole. The fish comes, frozen now, in bags, which is straightforward enough. The cooking is minimal: the whitebait are dredged in flour (devilled whitebait being tossed in flour heavily dusted with cayenne), plunged into hot fat, piled on a plate and served with deep-fried parsley, a squeeze of lemon (muslin-covered if we're being trad here) and brown bread and butter. Of course, the parsley in question is the old, curly kind (now curiously marketed, in seed packets at least, as 'afro parsley') which has long been awaiting rehabilitation.

vegetable oil for frying
500g bag whitebait
100g flour
salt and pepper

1 bunch flat-leaf parsley
Maldon salt
lemons for serving

Heat the oil for frying in a deep-fat fryer to about 190°C.

Put the whitebait and seasoned flour into a plastic bag, and toss everything around to coat the fish.

Shake off the excess flour by turning out the whole bag into a sieve, and then plunge the little fishes into the oil. Cook for about 3 minutes or until they look crispy and tempting – though I can see that for a squeamish generation, the idea of eating baby fish, whole, might not tempt. How wrong they are, if that's the case.

Turn them out onto kitchen towels, and while the fish are losing any excess oil (we want desirable crunch) throw in a small handful of parsley to deep fry; watch out, it will spit. (A splatter guard is useful. Not charming, but useful.) When it has turned a very dark green, drain it and serve it with the whitebait, well sprinkled with Maldon salt and surrounded with lemon wedges.

Serves 2 as a main course or 4 as a starter.

LIPTAUER

What did I get myself into, deciding to put this here? It sounds, or will do once I explain it, so unlikely, so culinarily yesteryear. But if we're talking family favourites I couldn't leave it out. Liptauer was *the* deli-counter delicacy of my childhood, and another eating-item I'd all but forgotten about. But something made me remember it and, from taste-memory and some notes from the kitchen book inherited by my friend Olivia from her mother, I tried my hand at making it myself, and I can confidently and categorically state that it's not some sentimental yearning that makes me now want to see its comeback. You don't need to go in for the retro-moulding here, just mix the ingredients and plonk them in a bowl if you like: but whatever, this glorious, cream-cheese, caper, caraway seed and paprika combination, spread over sour black bread or – if you don't have the genetic taste for it – over those hexagonal black charcoal biscuits which you can get from the supermarket, is rhapsodically unbeatable.

500g cream cheese
500g curd cheese
4–5 tablespoons capers
8 cornichons, chopped
3 teaspoons paprika, plus more for decoration
pinch of salt
good grating of black pepper

2 teaspoons caraway seeds
2 teaspoons French mustard
1-litre mould (optional)

for drizzling over:
1–2 tablespoons flavourless vegetable oil
fat pinch of paprika

Beat the two cheeses together until they are smooth, and then add all the other ingredients. Mix everything together well, and then turn into a small pudding basin or bowl with a capacity of approximately 2 pints, lined with clingfilm for easier unmoulding later (I give the imperial measure because my Tupperwares are so marked and besides, it is fitting here). Smooth the top with a spatula and cover with the overhanging clingfilm. Place it in the fridge to set. I put a couple of tins on top to press it down, but I don't feel it's crucial. I think it's because my mother was always putting pâtés and suchlike in the fridge with weights on.

When it has become cold enough to turn out – a few hours should do it – unwrap the folded-over clingfilm on top, place a plate over the now uncovered bowl, turn it the other way out and unmould. Pull the clingfilm off and drizzle over a rust-red ooze, made by mixing the oil with a pinch of paprika.

Serve this with black bread, black biscuits or poppy-seed-sprinkled bagels, gerkins and, if you like, some chopped red onions.

GRANNY LAWSON'S LUNCH DISH

When my paternal grandmother died recently, I got all her old, battered cookery note-books, and this is a recipe from one of them. In truth, I don't remember her cooking it ever, but then she took the decision relatively early on in my life that she got vertigo in the kitchen and therefore, in the interest of health you understand, cooked rarely. But I love these sorts of domestic diaries, half-filled with recipes torn out from papers, the rest a handwritten mixture of tips passed on by friends or accounts of lunches served to them. Cooking isn't just about ingredients, weights and measures: it's social history, personal history.

I love too the simplicity of its name as it appears in my grandmother's hand – just 'lunch dish'. And yes, I won't deny it has a retro-appeal – the chopped hard-boiled eggs and olives in the pie somehow even now convey the sense of adventurousness that a fifties' housewife would have had in making this – but it tastes fabulously good, hot or cold.

In cooking this, I altered things as I went along. For example, I have my way of making pastry (freezing the fat and flour together for 10 minutes before rubbing them in) and prefer to use Italian 00 flour which makes for a helpfully elastic dough, but that's part of what makes cooking alive. (Interestingly, though, the olive oil specified is not a contemporary addition but my grandmother's untampered-with injunction.) It has to be an improvisational rather than a formulaic activity. As with everything that matters in life, if it isn't honest, it's nothing.

If pastry seems daunting to you, then this is a good place to start, because it's a rough, ramshackle square of a thing: no fancy tins, no fancy techniques. That pleases me too: Frank Spencer here is always going to fare better freeform.

for the pastry:
250g plain flour, preferably Italian 00
50g hard vegetable fat, such as Cookeen
75g cold, unsalted butter
approx. 4 tablespoons (60ml) chilled, salted water
1 egg beaten with salt for brushing over

325g (2–3) tomatoes or same amount of drained, chopped, canned ones
200g (about 2 small) onions
2 eggs, hard-boiled
90g pitted black olives
2 tablespoons olive oil, not extra-virgin
250g organic minced beef
fat pinch allspice
salt and pepper

To make the pastry, measure the flour into a dish that will fit into the deep-freeze (it doesn't need to have a lid) and cut the Cookeen and butter into small – approx. 1cm – dice and toss them in the flour. Put in the deep-freeze for 10 minutes.

I tend to make pastry in my KitchenAid, but a processor's fine too. In whatever

contraption – fitted with the flat paddle in the one, with the double-bladed knife in the other – mix until you have a mixture that resembles coarse porridge oats. Now, dribble in the chilled salted water, slowly, with the motor still running, until the dough looks as if it's about to cohere, but stopping short of it's actually clumping totally. Turn out of the processor (though you could still do this in the bowl of the mixer) and squidge together with your hands until all the pastry forms a cohesive ball. Dribble in a little more water if you feel it needs it. Divide into two pieces of equal size and form into fat discs. Cover with clingfilm and leave in the fridge for 20 minutes. And this can be done a good day or two in advance if it helps.

Preheat the oven to 200°C/gas mark 6.

Put the tomatoes in a bowl, cover with boiling water from the kettle and leave for 5 minutes. Drain, run under the cold tap, then peel, de-seed and chop roughly (or use tinned tomatoes, chopped and drained). Peel and chop the onions, hard-boiled eggs and olives, too.

In a large frying pan over medium heat, warm the oil. Cook the chopped onions until softened and beginning to colour, turning the flame down to low if they look as if they're catching. Turn the heat back to medium and add the chopped tomatoes and cook, stirring for a minute or so before adding the mince. Stir well, breaking up the clumps of meat with your wooden spoon as you go, then, when the meat's browned, stir in the chopped eggs and olives and season with the allspice and salt and pepper. Cook over gentle heat for about 20 minutes, stirring occasionally.

Get a baking sheet out, and flour a surface and rolling pin. Remove the pastry from the fridge and roll out one of the discs until you have a thin, but not exaggeratedly so, rough square that will fit on the baking sheet, then place it on the sheet. Now roll out the second disc and leave it there while you cover the layer on the sheet with the minced-beef mixture, leaving a margin of about 3cm all around. With a bit of cold water and your fingers, dampen this edge. Place the second square of pastry on top and press the edges together to seal. Now, roll these edges back on themselves once or twice, then get a fork and press it, the tines curved-side down, against this rolled border. Prong the top of the pastry to make air holes and then beat the egg with a generous sprinkling of salt and brush the top and edges of the pie with it to glaze.

Put it in the oven for 20 minutes, by which time the pastry will be golden and cooked. Slice it into fat oblongs and eat warm with a vegetable or salad, or cold, wrapped in a napkin and without ceremony or cutlery.

Serves 6.

MY GRANDMOTHER'S GINGER-JAM
BREAD AND BUTTER PUDDING

This recipe comes from my maternal grandmother's recipe folder, a wonderfully retro piece of design, circa late sixties, early seventies. Bread and butter pudding has, I know, gone from stodgy disparagement to fashionable rehabilitation and back to not-that-again clichédom, but I am not prepared to let any of that bother me.

This version uses brown bread rather than white, and between the buttery sandwiches is heaped chunky-hot ginger jam, sometimes sold as ginger marmalade, but most usually, if quaintly, as ginger conserve; on top is sprinkled demerara sugar mixed with aromatically warm ground ginger, the spice of the old-fashioned English kitchen.

My grandmother, more austerely, used milk; I go for mostly cream: nothing creates so well that tender-bellied swell of softly set custard.

75g unsalted butter

75g sultanas

3 tablespoons dark rum

10 slices brown bread

approx. 10 x 15ml tablespoons ginger
**   conserve or marmalade**

4 egg yolks

1 egg

3 tablespoons caster sugar

500ml double cream

200ml full-fat milk

1 teaspoon ground ginger

2 tablespoons demerara sugar

Preheat the oven to 180°C/gas mark 4.

Grease a pudding dish with a capacity of about 1½ litres with some of the butter.

Put the sultanas in a small bowl, pour the rum over, and microwave them for 1 minute, then leave them to stand. This is a good way to soak them quickly but juicily.

Make sandwiches with the brown bread, butter and ginger jam (2 tablespoonfuls in each sandwich); you should have some butter left over to smear on the top later. Now cut the sandwiches in half into triangles and arrange them evenly along the middle of the pudding dish. I put one in the dish with the point of the sandwich upwards then one with flat-side uppermost, then with point-side uppermost and so on, then squeeze a sandwich-triangle down each side – but you do as you please. Sprinkle over the sultanas and unabsorbed rum that remains in the bowl.

Whisk the egg yolks and egg together with the caster sugar, and pour in the cream and milk. Pour this over the triangles of bread and leave them to soak up the liquid for about 10 minutes, by which time the pudding is ready to go into the oven. Smear the bread crusts that are poking out of the custard with the soft butter, mix the ground ginger and demerara sugar together and sprinkle this mixture on your buttered crusts and then lightly over the rest of the pudding.

Sit the pudding dish on a baking sheet and put in the oven to cook for about 45 minutes or until the custard has set and puffed up slightly. Remove, let sit for 10 minutes – by which time the puffiness will have deflated somewhat – and spoon out into bowls, putting a jug of custard, should you so wish, on the table to be served alongside.

Serves 6.

CUSTARD

If you are going to eat this sort of pudding, it can't hurt to know how to make the custard to go with it. It is useful to know, that you need 1 egg yolk for each 100ml of milk or cream. It's harder to be precise about the sugar, which depends on your taste, what you're eating the custard with, and whether it's going to be hot or cold.

1 vanilla pod or 1 teaspoon vanilla extract
500ml single cream, or half milk, half cream

5 large egg yolks
1 tablespoon caster sugar

Half-fill the sink with cold water.

If you've got a vanilla pod, cut it lengthways so that the seeds will be released, and heat it in a pan with the single cream till nearly boiling. Take off the heat, cover and leave to steep for 20 minutes. If you're not using a pod, put the cream and vanilla extract on the heat, and beat the egg yolks and sugar together in a bowl. When the cream's warm, pour it over the sweet yolks, beating all the while. Pour the uncooked custard back into the rinsed-out and dried pan and cook over a medium heat, stirring constantly, until the custard's thickened. Ten minutes should do it, unless you're being very timorous and leaving the flame too low. When the custard's thickened, plunge the pan into the cold water in the sink and whisk it for a minute or so. You can eat it straight away, or if you want to make it in advance, reheat later in a bowl over a pan of simmering water.

Serves 4.

CHOCOLATE-CHESTNUT REFRIGERATOR CAKE

This is another of my maternal grandmother's recipes and in truth reminds me much more of her than the bread and butter pudding. I've changed it a bit, not least substituting dark rum for her juice and zest of an orange and a slug or two of Grand Marnier. It's not that I didn't like her version, but it was just a bit too much like a homespun Terry's chocolate orange for comfort. You do as you please.

This is very much a period offering: from a time of fridge-cooked loaves of things, sliced at dinner parties and served with dainty fruit salads (my grandmother suggested some sliced oranges here, which is of a piece), but it nevertheless resolutely deserves a place on the contemporary table. It's incredibly easy to make, and dangerously compelling to eat, one of those puddings about which everyone says 'it's very rich' before going on to third helpings.

I think it needs a smooth, sour blob of crème fraîche alongside: it *is* sweet; but the crystallised violets you see adorning the slice opposite are just a sentimental touch. My grandmother loved them, as did my mother – they are, as it happens, the traditional sprinkling accompaniment to monte bianco, that gunge-heavy mixture of cream, chocolate, rum and chestnut purée that – more free-form, less prinked – my mother went in for.

500g (2 tins) sweetened chestnut purée
175g soft, unsalted butter
300g dark chocolate, minimum 70%
  cocoa solids
3 tablespoons dark rum

to serve:
crème fraîche
crystallised violets

Beat the purée in a bowl until it's smooth, and then add the butter, beating again to make a well-blended mixture.

Melt the chocolate and let it cool slightly, before adding it to the chestnut and butter in the bowl. Beat in the rum, and spoon the chocolate mixture into a 23 x 10cm loaf tin, lined with clingfilm, in two batches, making sure the first layer reaches the corners and sides of the bottom of the tin before you smooth over the rest. Wrap the overhanging clingfilm over the cake so that it is completely covered, and put it in the fridge to set for at least four hours, but a day or so in advance if you want.

Don't take the loaf tin out of the fridge until you want to eat it, when you just unmould the cake, cut it into thin slices and serve with crème fraîche or sour cream.

Makes 10–12 slices.

NOTES

NOTES

CHAPTER EIGHT

SUPPERTIME

There is a way of inviting friends over for dinner without hating them, yourself, the kitchen and the world. Cooking isn't performance art – or shouldn't be. Perhaps it's unrealistic to hope to be a model of serenity throughout, but if you can manage to relax, both the food and the evening will be better. The answer is to cook in a way that doesn't involve huge amounts of effort or time. Ease yourself into a repertoire, make the food welcoming rather than fussy and remember that it's not a test of your worth and acceptability: it's just dinner.

THREE-COURSE DINNER FOR 8

Salmon with ginger, soy and rice vinegar

Bream with anchovies, thyme and chick peas; and Egyptian tomato salad

Chocolate pots

I don't, as a rule, always bother with starters, but sometimes you want to go in for a fully-fledged dinner party. By that I don't mean that you have to start folding your napkins into fancy shapes or pushing yourself beyond all known gastronomic boundaries. However important food is, it's a part of life, not the whole point of it. A good dinner party is one where people enjoy themselves: the last thing you want is a tense and hallowed silence to descend as you, exhausted, slump some perfect creation on the table, desperate for their approval and admiration. The food – and the drink – are there to give rise to, not upstage, conversation and companiability.

This dinner is eminently do-able without your having to devote the best part of two days to cooking it. Certainly, some of the food is fiddled about with, in a low-effort kind of a way, in advance, but that's just to make life easier on the night.

SALMON WITH GINGER, SOY AND RICE VINEGAR

This is a very easy starter, not least because no cooking is involved at all. All you need to do is mix the first four ingredients, leave them to steep for 10 minutes or so in a jug (longer if it helps), arrange the salmon slices on a couple of large plates and then pour the liquid over before scattering with some finely chopped spring onions.

I get the salmon from the fishmonger and ask them to do the fiddly slicing, but otherwise you could use the rag-like salmon escalopes some supermarkets sell. And if the idea of raw salmon appals you, simply flash fry the escalopes, transfer briskly to waiting plates, slice them into wide strips then pour over the gingery juices and serve either as is, still warm, or left to cool to room temperature.

This is also wonderful made with sliver-thin slices of tuna.

60ml Kikkoman soy sauce
60ml rice vinegar
3cm ginger peeled and grated (preferably with a Microplane grater)
1 tablespoon toasted sesame oil (optional)

750g salmon, preferably organic, sliced as thinly as smoked salmon, or as near to that as possible
2–4 spring onions, finely sliced

Mix the soy sauce and rice vinegar together and grate in the ginger. If you want to add the sesame oil, do – its aromatic nuttiness adds a rounded mellowness – but salmon is oily enough not to need it, so leave it out if you want something a little more delicately astringent.

Cut the very thin salmon pieces (and I use kitchen scissors for this) into wide strips and arrange them any old how on a couple of plates. Pour over the gingery dressing and scatter the finely sliced spring onions on top.

Now was that hard?

BREAM WITH ANCHOVIES AND THYME

May I make a suggestion? Please don't tell people that the sauce has anchovy in it. What comes through is not fishiness, but a robust, rounded saltiness. So many people have an anti-anchovy prejudice that it's hardly worth the explaining: deception, I've found, is the more sensible route. I use anchovy fillets that have been stored in an olive-oil-filled jar, though a squirt of anchovy paste from a tube is a perfectly respectable substitute.

I make a version of this sauce a lot, with a variety of fish, mostly white; but I ought to tell you it also makes a wonderful sauce for lamb (in which case replace the sherry with red wine). The chick peas, below, are perfect with the fish or lamb variant too. And the useful thing is that with all the meaty pulsiness of them, you don't need to bother with potatoes. (And although I've given the recipe for the chick peas after this, the main course, you do need to get on and cook them first. Be warned.)

Red bream (sometimes called redfish, though generally known abroad as Norwegian Haddock) which is common to our shores is not quite the same – and certainly a lot cheaper – than the seabream caught in warmer waters. It's perhaps not quite as delicate, but there is a fleshy firmness that makes these chunky fillets stand up well to robust flavours. And the pearl-pink skin, like the flash of a Barbie mermaid's tail, is quite beautiful.

2–4 tablespoons olive oil, plus dribble of oil from anchovies	**2 anchovy fillets**
12 fillets of red bream, skin on	**leaves from a few sprigs of thyme**
1 clove garlic, minced	**2 tablespoons sherry**
	1 fat knob unsalted butter (approx. 15g)

In a large, non-stick frying pan (I use a Woll fish pan here) pour a little olive oil and, when warm, start frying the fish. They won't need much, but keep an eye – some fillets may be thicker than others – and remove to a couple of warm plates, tented with foil, as they're cooked. I think these look best with the pearly pink skin uppermost.

When all the fish fillets are cooked, add a tablespoon of olive oil plus the dribble of anchovy oil to the pan and stir in the minced garlic and the anchovy fillets. Keep stirring with a wooden spoon or spatula and, as the oil warms, the garlic should soften and the anchovies seem to melt into a sauce. Add most of the thyme leaves, then the sherry. After a scant minute's bubbling, replace the wooden spoon in your hand with a magiwhisk – one of my favourite pieces of equipment – and, off the heat, whisk in the butter. Pour this small amount of viscous sauce over the two plates of fish (this is for flavouring, not coverage) then sprinkle with the few remaining thyme leaves. Serve with the chick peas and tomato salad. I know this sounds like a lot for 8, but I like to work on making enough for half those present to have second helpings. At any rate, I've found that a good rule of thumb.

CHICK PEAS WITH CHILLI, GARLIC AND THYME

This is the chick pea recipe I return to again and again, with some variation in herbs used; here I've added thyme for aromatic balance with the fish, above. If it helps, replace the fresh thyme with dried thyme (as long as it isn't stale and years old) and the fresh red chilli with a dried hot chilli pepper.

There are three things I feel you should know about chick peas. The first is that they need longer soaking than anyone tells you (24 hours for preference); the second is that they take longer to cook than anyone tells you (1½–2 hours is what you should be reckoning on); and the third is that they will be more buttery, velvety and nuttily tender than you could ever imagine if you make up Anna del Conte's paste of flour, bicarb and salt and add it to the soaking water.

I know long soaking and long cooking make these chick peas seem a bit of a palaver, but nothing's hard, in the first place, and what I find makes life generally easier is that you can cook them in advance. This means that all you really need to do on the night is make the tomato salad, heat up the chick peas, or turn them in the chilli and so forth, quickly fry the fish and you're away. So in fact, despite lengthy (but not tricky) preparation, this makes for a swiftly and easily assembled drop-dead dinner.

500g chick peas
2 tablespoons flour
2 tablespoons salt
2 teaspoons bicarbonate of soda

1 onion, halved (don't bother to peel it)
6 or so sprigs of thyme
60ml olive oil (not extra-virgin)
Maldon salt

1 red chilli pepper
1 onion
2 fat cloves garlic
leaves from 4–5 sprigs of thyme
60ml olive oil (not extra-virgin)
Maldon salt
good slug extra-virgin olive oil

Soak the chick peas in enough cold water to cover generously and make a paste up with the flour, salt and bicarb and a little more cold water. Add this to the soaking chick peas (I just dunk in the bowl I've mixed it up in). Leave for 24 hours.

Drain and thoroughly rinse the chick peas in a colander under running cold water in the sink. Tip them into a large saucepan, cover abundantly with cold water and add the halved onion, sprigs of thyme and olive oil. Do not salt: at this stage it would make the skins tough. Put on a lid, bring to the boil and let bubble away for an hour and a half. At this stage only may you take off the lid to see how cooked the chick peas are; you may also now add salt. If they're cooked, you should lower in a measuring jug to remove about 500ml of the cooking water; otherwise keep going until they're ready.

Once you've reserved your chick-pea cooking liquid, drain the chick peas and remove – with tongs for ease – the bits of onion and thyme. This doesn't have to be ruthlessly carried out, but just get rid of any obvious bits. Once cold you can Tupperware the chick peas, tossing them first in olive oil to prevent drying, until you need them; or else cook them through to the final stage, let them cool and refrigerate them in a covered container or clingfilmed bowl.

Roughly seed and chop the red chilli pepper, peel and chunk the onion, press on the garlic cloves to loosen, then remove the skins, bung everything, along with the thyme leaves, into the processor and blitz to a pulp. In a large, deep frying pan or casserole – whatever suits – pour the oil and, when warm, tip in the pulp from the processor. Sprinkle with salt and cook gently, stirring occasionally, for 5–10 minutes or until soft. Add the chick peas and turn to coat, then pour in about half the chick-pea cooking liquid and bring to a bubble. Put on a lid and let cook gently till the chick peas are hot and soft; you will probably need to remove the lid at the end of cooking to let excess water evaporate. If, however, you run out of liquid before the chick peas are tender and soused enough, simply add more of the reserved water.

When the chick peas are ready, turn into a large bowl, or keep in the pan in which you've cooked them, and add extra-virgin olive oil: drizzle then stir and keep going until the chick peas are glossy but not too thickly slicked. Sprinkle over Maldon salt and some thyme leaves if you feel like it (and happen to have some scattered anyway over the worksurface – you might well at this stage) or leave them simply oiled and salted.

EGYPTIAN TOMATO SALAD

I found this salad in a lovely little book – 'a memoir with recipes' – called *Apricots on the Nile*, by Colette Rossant. And although it sounds a lot of bother blanching and peeling the tomatoes, all in fact it involves is leaving the tomatoes for a few minutes in a bowlful of just-boiled water, after which their skins will come off without any trouble. It is worth doing this: the tomatoes will be more seductively tender and the nubbly dressing then permeates them better.

If a shallot is beyond you, use the white parts of two or three spring onions.

1 shallot, peeled
1 clove of garlic, peeled
3–4 tablespoons olive oil
salt and pepper

5 medium-sized vine tomatoes (approx.
    750g altogether)
good squeeze of lemon juice
Maldon salt
handful freshly chopped chervil

Chop the shallot and garlic as finely as is humanly possible – or just blitz to a pulp in a processor – and put in a small bowl with the oil, a pinch of salt and a grinding of pepper, and leave to steep while you blanche the tomatoes: that's to say, put them in a large bowl then pour boiling water over them so that they are hotly submerged. Leave for 5 minutes then tip into a colander and run under cold water. Using a sharp knife, peel off the skins (which is now easy), then cut these fuzzy spheres into slices, as thick or as thin as you like (I like them somewhere in the middle). Arrange the tomatoes in a dish and pour over the dressing, using your fingers to mix well. I find it easier to use one bowl for steeping purposes and another one, later, for serving. You can let the tomatoes sit like this for a good couple of hours. Yes, some liquid will collect, but the flavours will deepen wonderfully.

When you're ready to eat, either leave the dressed tomatoes in the bowl or decant to a new one, but either way, using your hands, turn them to coat, squeeze over some lemon juice, and sprinkle with Maldon salt and a tablespoon or so of freshly chopped chervil. Use another herb if you like, but there is one inflexible rule governing this salad: it must be served at room temperature. Leave it in the fridge until the last minute and all will be lost.

CHOCOLATE POTS

Despite my antipathy for the ramekin-bound and single-portioned, I make no apology for these. Partly, I suppose, it's nostalgia: when I was a child, these dense, dark, just-solid offerings, known more familiarly then by the French tag, *petits pots aux chocolats*, were the dernier cri in bistro chic. Then they were served, as they still are in France, in small white amphora-shaped vessels, small urns with their curved handles, in relief, tilting upwards towards the expectant eater. There's nothing to stop you using them now; I would if I weren't so sold on the Polystyrene cups recast in porcelain that you see opposite. The silky chocolate mixture contained within them is just mousse without the whisked egg whites, easier to make and somehow less vulgar, for all the daintiness of their presentation.

The method used to make them is ludicrously simply and done, necessarily, in advance. You just process the lot, pour them into small containers (coffee cups would be fine: there's no need to make a production out of it) and sit them in the fridge to set. I stumbled across this method in one of Nick Nairn's books. He, in turn, got it from Hilaire Walden. I've tinkered somewhat with the traditional flavours, adding spices to bring to this the aromatic richness of Mexican hot chocolate (or so I, in my unfounded fantasy, like to think) which tempers the uncompromising richness of the confection without losing its seductive intensity.

175g best quality dark chocolate, minimum 70% cocoa solids
150ml double cream
100ml full-fat milk

½ teaspoon real vanilla extract
¼ teaspoon allspice
1 egg
8 x 60ml pots

Crush the chocolate to smithereens in the food processor. Heat the cream and milk until just about boiling, add the vanilla and allspice and pour through the funnel over the chocolate. Let stand for 30 seconds. Process for 30 seconds, then crack the egg down the funnel and process for 45 seconds.

Pour into whatever little cups you're serving in, and sit them in the fridge for 6 hours or overnight. But remember to take them out of the fridge a good 20 minutes before you want them to be eaten; the chill interferes with their luscious, silky richness.

This makes 500ml altogether: enough to fill 8 little pots of approximately 60ml. But if you've got only bigger cups, just augment quantities.

Aromatic lamb-shank stew with couscous
Crème brûlée

The specification that this is a kitchen supper holds only notional weight: along with most people in the country, I have no dining room. The gracious option is one, then, not open to me. So what I mean here is a dinner party that concentrates on getting friends round the table and feeding them well. There's no starter, the main course is a vast bowlful of unkempt stew; pudding, however elegant, comes in one big dish, to be plonked down and dug into unceremoniously.

AROMATIC LAMB-SHANK STEW

Don't let the word stew put you off. Yes, I know it's crippled with connotations of school-dinner gristle and gluey-gravied mess, but the lamb shanks here are anything but that. Of course, you could use shoulder, cut into greed-satisfying chunks, and it still wouldn't be compromise, but the bone in the shank gives such rounded richness of flavour and there's something so unpretentiously satisfying about the great meaty hunkiness of it on the plate. Since supermarkets now routinely stock (or will order in) lamb shanks, and since they're both meaty and cheap, it makes sense to seek them out for this.

The spicing, the muddy softening of the lentils within, owe something to Moroccan cooking, but only obliquely. I've used the seasonings – Marsala, soy – I have regularly to hand (unlike restaurant chefs, I don't re-kit my non-existent pantry for each new recipe) to bring to it the mellow depth I want to find.

As with all stews, this is even better made in advance and reheated; for me, this only makes things easier. The couscous, however, needs to be made last minute. If you don't own a couscoussier (and there's no reason why you should) just steam these grains above boiling water in an ordinary vegetable steamer. Of course it's possible to cook couscous just by steeping it in boiling water (and check packet instructions for directions) but I can't honestly tell you it will make them as fluffily light.

Otherwise, with this aromatic, sauce-rich stew, just serve plain rice – or a bowlful of buttery mash, of half potatoes, half parsnips, well seasoned and spiced with mace.

6 tablespoons groundnut or vegetable oil

8 lamb shanks

2 onions

4 cloves of garlic

sprinkling of salt

1 tablespoon turmeric

1 teaspoon ground ginger

1 dried red chilli pepper, crumbled, or
 ¼ teaspoon dried chilli flakes

2 teaspoons cinnamon

¼ teaspoon freshly grated
 nutmeg

black pepper

3 tablespoons honey

1 tablespoon soy sauce

3 tablespoons Marsala

6 tablespoons red lentils

to serve:

3 tablespoons chopped pistachios,
 chopped blanched almonds or a
 mixture of both

Put 3 tablespoons of the oil into a very large, wide, heavy-bottomed pan and warm over medium heat. Brown the lamb shanks, in batches, in the pan and then remove to a roasting tin or whatever else you've got to hand to sit them in.

Peel the onions and garlic and process in a food processor or chop them finely by hand. Add the remaining oil to the pan, and fry the onion-garlic mush until soft, sprinkling salt over to stop it catching.

Stir in the turmeric, ground ginger, chilli, cinnamon and nutmeg, and season with some freshly ground pepper. Stir again, adding the honey, soy sauce and Marsala. Put the shanks back in the pan, add cold water almost to cover, bring to the boil then put a lid on the pan, lower the heat and simmer very gently for 1–1½ hours or until the meat is tender.

Add the red lentils and cook for about 20 minutes longer without the lid, until the lentils have softened into the sauce, and the juices have reduced and thickened slightly. Check for seasoning.

Toast the nuts by heating them for a few minutes in a dry frying pan, and sprinkle onto the lamb as you serve it.

Serves 6.

COUSCOUS

The lamb shanks can be cooked in advance: this, as I've said, needs to be done at the last minute. But relax, it's a low-effort undertaking.

500g couscous

2 teaspoons salt

4 cardamom pods

approx. 25g unsalted butter in two slices

25g flaked almonds

50g pine nuts

25g pistachios

Fill the bottom of a steamer, or base of a couscoussier should you possess one, with water and bring to the boil. When it looks like it's almost ready to boil, fill the kettle and put it on, then empty the couscous into a glass bowl, add the salt, crush in the cardamom and mix with your fingers, then pour over a litre of boiling water from the kettle and place a plate on top of the bowl. Leave to stand for 5 minutes, then drain and empty into the steamer or couscoussier top and sit this on top of the boiling water beneath. Add the slices of butter on top of the couscous then clamp on the lid and let steam for 7–10 minutes, by which time the couscous should be tenderly cooked and the butter melting. (You can do this a simpler way if you prefer, by just steeping the couscous in the boiling water for 10–15 minutes, but the grains will be more dense and more likely to clump. It's not disastrous, however, and you must decide what you're prepared to do.)

Meanwhile, toast the almonds by frying them in a dry pan till fragrant and golden, remove them to a plate, then do the same to the pine nuts. Chop the pistachios. Once the couscous is cooked, tip into a bowl, fork through (and always use a fork for mixing or fluffing up couscous; a spoon will crush it and turn it stodgy), sprinkling in the almonds and pine nuts as you do so (and taste for seasoning at the same time, too). Now fork in most of the pistachios, and sprinkle those that remain lightly on top.

CREME BRULEE

The first thing you should know about crème brûlée is that it's not hard to make. And few puddings are as voluptuously, seductively easy to eat. I never make mine in little individual ramekins (though there's nothing to stop you if that's what you prefer) but in one large dish: there is something so welcoming about a big bowlful, the rich, smooth, eggy cream waiting to ooze out on the spoon that breaks through the tortoiseshell disc on top.

You don't need me to tell you about the blowtorch bit; this has been rehearsed enough. But it isn't a gimmick or a gratuitous act of showmanship: just the best way of burning the sprinkled-over sugar to instant, brittle compactness. You can get a blowtorch now from more or less any kitchen shop; and there's something curiously satisfying about wielding it.

600ml double cream
1 vanilla pod
8 egg yolks

3 tablespoons caster sugar
approx. 6 tablespoons demerara sugar

Put a pie dish of about 20cm diameter in the freezer for at least 20 minutes. Half-fill the sink with cold water. This is just a precaution in case the custard looks as if it's about to split, in which case you should plunge the pan into the water and whisk the custard. I'm not saying it will – with so many egg yolks in the rich cream, it thickens quickly and easily enough – but I always feel better if I've done this.

Put the cream and vanilla pod into a saucepan and bring to boiling point, but do not let boil. Beat the eggs and caster sugar together in a bowl, and, still beating, pour the flavoured cream over it, pod and all. Rinse and dry the pan and pour the custard mix back in. Cook over medium heat (or low, if you're scared) until the custard thickens: about 10 minutes should do it. You do want this to be a good, voluptuous crème, so don't err on the side of runny caution. Remember, you've got your sinkful of cold water to plunge the pan into should it really look as if it's about to split.

When the cream's thick enough, take out the vanilla pod, retrieve the pie dish and pour this crème into the severely chilled container. Leave to cool, then put in the fridge till truly cold. Sprinkle with demerara sugar, spoonful by spoonful, and burn with a blowtorch till you have a blistered tortoiseshell covering on top.

Put back in the fridge if you want, but remember to take it out a good 20 minutes before serving. At which stage, put the bowl on the table and, with a large spoon and unchecked greed, crack through the sugary carapace and delve into the satin-velvet, vanilla-speckled cream beneath. No more talking: just eat.

NOTES

NOTES

_____

_____

_____

_____

_____

_____

_____

_____

_____

_____

_____

_____

_____

_____

_____

_____

CHAPTER NINE

SLOW-COOK WEEKEND

The point about weekend food is not that you've got more time to cook it, but that you've got more time to eat it. I like to do the sort of cooking that gets on with itself slowly, so that I can potter about the house unencumbered and invite people to lunch without having to slave from first thing in the morning. Most of all, the food shouldn't be about performance and high-strive presentation, but about lingered-over plenty.

SATURDAY LUNCH FOR 6–8

Warm shredded lamb salad with mint and pomegranate
Red peppers with crumbled feta and almonds
Turkish Delight syllabub

This is – give or take – a regular kitchen fall-back position for me on Saturdays. It can be streamlined or amplified to suit how I feel and who's coming, but the main thing is that most of the food is prepared either in advance or without strenuous effort. Most times, if it's lunch, I wouldn't go full out with pudding, but just buy huge wedges of two or three cheeses, maybe leaving the feta on the peppers out of the equation, and let people pick their way to a languorous conclusion. And this is the point of this sort of meal: it is about mood, pace, companionship. Why else are you going to be cooking for people?

WARM SHREDDED LAMB SALAD WITH MINT AND POMEGRANATE

The virtue of this is that you can cook the lamb overnight, which means all you need to do is shred the meat, dress it and make the salads at lunchtime itself. Or put it in the oven at a slightly higher temperature, but still unfrenetically low, in the morning and fiddle about as people arrive. You do need to serve the lamb salad warm rather than cold (a bit of fat provides flavoursome lubrication at anything above room temperature; once cold we're talking congealed, waxy whiteness – not such an attractive proposition), but if you keep the lamb tented with foil once it's out of the oven – should you need to hold it for longer than an hour or two – that shouldn't pose problems.

If it's not the pomegranate season you have a choice: either use pomegranate molasses (a tablespoonful or so, diluted with an equal amount of water) which you can get at some supermarkets now, or just use lemon juice and maybe even a little very-finely-grated zest.

1 shoulder of lamb (approx. 2½ kg)	Maldon salt
4 shallots, halved but not peeled	500ml boiling water
6 cloves garlic	small handful freshly chopped mint
1 carrot, peeled and halved	1 pomegranate

Preheat the oven to 140°C/gas mark 1.

On the hob, brown the lamb, fat-side down, in a large roasting tin. Remove when nicely browned across its middle (you won't get much more than this) and set aside while you fry the vegetables briefly. Just tip them into the pan – you won't need to add any more fat – and cook them, sprinkled with the salt, gently for a couple of minutes. Pour the water over and then replace the lamb, this time fat-side up. Let the liquid in the pan come to a bubble, then tent with foil and put in the preheated oven.

Now just leave it there while you sleep. I find that if I put the lamb in before I go to bed, it's perfect by lunchtime the next day. But the point is, at this temperature, nothing's going to go wrong with the lamb if you cook it for a little less or a little more.

If you want to cook the lamb the day you're going to eat it, heat the oven to 170°C/gas mark 3 and give it 5 hours or so. The point is to find a way of cooking that suits you: you know what sort of pottering relaxes you and what makes you feel constrained; how much time you've got, and how you want to use it. Don't let the food, the kitchen or the imagined expectations of other people bully you.

With that homily over, about an hour before you want to eat, remove the lamb from the tin to a large plate or carving board – not that it needs carving; the deal here is that it's unfashionably overcooked, falling to tender shreds at the touch of a fork. This is the best way to deal with shoulder of lamb: it's cheaper than leg, and the flavour is deeper, better, truer, but even good carvers, which I most definitely am not, can get unstuck trying to slice it.

I get on with the peppers while the lamb's sitting meekly, but you could equally have done this earlier, too (and see below for instructions). But to finish the lamb salad, simply pull it to pieces with a couple of forks on a large plate. Sprinkle with more Maldon salt and some freshly chopped mint, then cut the pomegranate in half and dot with the seeds from one of the halves. This is easily done; there's a simple trick, which means you never have to think of winkling out the jewelled pips with a safety pin every again. Simply hold the pomegranate half above the plate, take a wooden spoon and start bashing the curved skin side with it. Nothing will happen for a few seconds, but have faith. In a short while the glassy red, juicy beads will start raining down.

Take the other half and squeeze the preposterously pink juices over the warm shredded meat. Take to the table and serve.

What I do with the leftovers is warm a pitta bread in the microwave, and then spread it with a greedy dollop of hummus, then take the chill off the fridged lamb in the microwave (and see notes on cold fat, above) and stuff the already gooey pitta with it. Add freshly chopped mint, black pepper and whatever else you like; raw, finely chopped red onion goes dangerously well.

PEPPERS WITH FETA AND ALMONDS

This is really a vegetarian take on that classic combination of charred, peeled peppers and anchovies. And if it makes little sense in talking about a vegetarian version when this is paired with the lamb salad, above, then let me reassure you that there is no need to do it all. This pepper and feta combo, with a rocket (or other green) salad, some griddled aubergines dressed, as with the lamb above, with pomegranate and mint (or if you're not feeling up to that, just a bowl of good shop-bought hummus) and a pile of warmed pitta breads, would make the perfect Saturday lunch, vegetarians or no.

8 red or yellow peppers or a mixture of both

100g feta (or 200g if not serving the lamb)

couple of squeezes lemon juice

1 tablespoon extra-virgin olive oil

75g blanched or flaked almonds

2 tablespoons freshly chopped parsley

Peeling peppers is a time-consuming and fiddly job, but it isn't difficult – and this is a distinction that's important to remember. Like most tasks of this order, culinary or otherwise, the space it takes up in your head is greater than the actual demands of the activity, but if the idea of charring and then peeling eight peppers really appals, then don't do it. The world is not going to fall apart if you buy a jar of ready-peeled and oil-softened peppers, nor do you lose the right to occupy your own kitchen if you ignore my suggestion altogether. Make a tomato salad; buy some tabbouleh from the deli.

But meanwhile at stately Wayne mansion, preheat the grill as hot as you can get it, and then sit the peppers on a rack below. When the skin turns black and blistery, turn them; you want to char them on every side. You can do this also, if you've got a gas cooker, just by holding them with a long fork over the hob, but it can get tiresome to say the least.

When the peppers are black and charred, remove them (trying not to burn your-self) to a large bowl and cover immediately with clingfilm. Leave for 10–20 minutes.

Then uncover and, one by one, peel and de-seed the peppers. Don't get worried if the odd bit of skin (or indeed pip) remains. Cut or tear into wide chunks/strips (I don't like this too dinky) and arrange on a large plate. Crumble over the feta, then squeeze over lemon juice and drizzle with oil. Scatter over the almonds and sprinkle on the pars-ley – and that, frankly, is it.

Leftovers can be stuffed into pitta breads, as with the lamb, above, but the sweet, salty mix is also lovely as a sauce for pasta (better without the almonds, though I'd bet they'd all be picked off anyway by the time you got to leftover stage). Cook some penne, reserve a coffee-cupful of the cooking water on draining, then toss the pasta back into the hot pan with half the reserved water and a small bowlful of peppers and feta. Toss around so that everything begins to cohere (but not actually cook) and turn into a bowl. Eat.

TURKISH DELIGHT SYLLABUB

This hasn't got the temple-aching sweetness of Turkish Delight, nor its palate-cleaving glutinousness, but rather it is a cloud-light spoon-pudding version which attempts to catch its aromatic essence – perfect after the lamb and pomegranate salad above. That it requires no cooking, merely some pouring and whisking, doesn't hurt either.

I use Cointreau here, simply because I have an enormous bottle of it and I prefer not to have to whip out to the shops every time I want to make something, but if you've got any other drink which you feel would make a suitable base, then feel free to use it in its stead.

The quantities below make enough syllabub to fill, billowingly, eight 150ml glasses; I give spoon measures before the metric ones just because it makes the whole operation more relaxed if you dispense with weighing and measuring. And the vague amount of cream specified is just meant to indicate one of those old-pint tubs which hasn't been properly made metric, and therefore is a strange measurement.

12 tablespoons Cointreau (approx. 175ml)

juice of 2 lemons

8 tablespoons (approx. 125g) caster sugar

just under 600ml double cream

2 tablespoons rosewater

2 tablespoons orangeflower water

2 tablespoons pistachios, finely chopped

Combine the Cointreau, lemon juice and sugar in a large bowl (I use the bowl of my KitchenAid mixer) and stir to dissolve the sugar, or as good as. Slowly stir in the cream then get whisking. As I said, I use my freestanding mixer for this, but if you haven't got one, don't worry – but I would then advise a hand-held electric mixer. This takes *ages* to thicken and doing it by hand will drive you demented with tedium and impatience. Or it would me.

When the cream's fairly thick, but still not thick enough to hold its shape, dribble in the flower waters and then keep whisking until you have a creamy mixture that's light and airy but able to form soft peaks. I always think of syllabub as occupying some notional territory between solid and liquid; you're aiming, as you whisk, for what Jane Grigson called 'bulky whiteness'. Whatever: better slightly too runny than slightly too thick, so proceed carefully, but don't get anxious about it. You can anyway probably see the texture it is from the picture, opposite.

Spoon the syllabub in airy dollops into small glasses, letting the mixture billow up above the rim of the glass, and scatter finely chopped pistachios on top. In *How to Eat*, there's a recipe for pistachio crescents which would be fabulous dunked into and eaten with this. But only if you feel like it: the cool, fool-like smoothness of this is perfect as it is.

SUNDAY LUNCH FOR 12

**Slow-roasted shoulder of aromatic pork with creamy potato gratin
and stir-braised Savoy cabbage with nigella seeds
Easy sticky-toffee pudding**

You are just going to have to believe me when I tell you that there is such a thing as a lazy Sunday lunch for twelve and, keep calm, I propose you cook it. The reason you should believe me is that I am not someone who churns out vats of food without the merest furrowing of a brow or clenching of a knuckle. True, I like cooking, and I like my friends, but having to feed too many of them in my kitchen at one time can turn me into someone positively curdled with resentment and panic. I'd like to be calm, I'd like to be unflappable, but some things are just never going to come to pass.

So, working along the premise of change what you can and accept what you can't, I've found a way of cooking that satisfies my need to be hospitable while accommodating my hostessly shortcomings. The first imperative is that there should be a great deal, indeed too much, to eat. It might sound blasphemous to say that my Jewish-mother leanings are best satisfied by the roasting of a whole shoulder of pork, but I'm afraid I've found this to be the case. The fact that this great weight of pig needs hardly any interference from you while it cooks satisfies the second requirement, namely that you are not working yourself up into a lather during the little free time you might have. But it's not quite as unsatisfying as that sounds: before you put the pork into the oven (where you leave it for a full day) you smother it with a fragrant paste of your own making, thereby giving yourself some essential element of kitchen pottering, without which you may as well be pinging the microwave, psychologically speaking.

Without wishing to sound like Marie-Antoinette, I do feel that pork does have to be the very best pork to start off with, not bred to flabby leanness in some godforsaken pig-penitentiary. These days this can be harder than it sounds. So I hope you'll thank me for telling you where this miracle-meat can be found, and moreover that you don't even need to go shopping for it yourself. You just phone Heritage Prime on 01297 489304 and throw yourself on Denise's mercy. Their pork, from a farm near Lyme Regis, is so much better than any pork you've ever tasted or could ever hope to taste. To say it's organic just tells you what isn't in it. What they add at Heritage Prime is immense care, good feed and excellent conditions. This does mean the meat costs more than you'd pay at the supermarket, but it isn't profiteering, it's because it's much more expensive to farm and rear animals like this. I'm not suggesting you spend more than you can, but with meat particularly – as we've learnt, or are beginning to learn, surely – it's better to buy the best occasionally, than the disreputably cut-price often. And don't necessarily disdain your local butcher, if you're lucky enough to have one still; indeed if you don't go to your butcher ever, there soon won't be any left to go to.

Once, with my order, Denise sent me a photo of 'the girls' on the bluebell-flecked hill overlooking Lyme Bay, which I stuck on my fridge. And although I realise it might sound macabre to some of you to be gazing at a picture of live pigs while cooking a dead one, I actually think it is a whole lot healthier than buying sanitised packets of clingfilmed meat from the supermarket that pretends to have no relationship with its source. Tastes a whole lot better, too.

The paste I spread on this pork is made of ginger, garlic, chilli and sherry vinegar, which has a Chinesey tone to it. Indeed, the pork when it's finished – the crackling glazed and crisp, the flesh beneath melting and to be torn rather than carved – reminds me obscurely of Peking duck. There's the same mixture of velvet-tender meat and seared-crisp skin.

SLOW-ROASTED AROMATIC SHOULDER OF PORK

I first got the idea of cooking a shoulder of pork over 24 hours like this from the second *River Café Cookbook*; my take on it is really a de-Italianised version. Any mixture of herbs or spices you want would do: this isn't a recipe so much as a suggestion.

1 shoulder of pork, skin scored (approx. 9½ kg) and see above

6 garlic cloves

1cm length of fresh ginger

2 fresh red chillies or 1 teaspoon dried red chilli flakes

3 tablespoons olive oil (not extra-virgin)

4 tablespoons sherry or rice vinegar

The pork takes 24 hours to cook, which is no cause for alarm, because for about 23 hours and 55 minutes you are ignoring it absolutely. And it makes your house smell like a home should.

So, if you're planning to eat this for Sunday lunch, at about Saturday lunchtime, preheat your (clean) oven to the hottest it will go. Sit the pork skinside up on a rack over a roasting tin. I like to use a pestle and mortar to make my paste because it makes me feel good, but you could just grate the garlic and ginger (one of my beloved, and often mentioned, Microplane graters is the tool for the job) and stir in chilli flakes, a tablespoonful of oil and two of vinegar if you want. Otherwise, pound together the peeled chopped ginger and peeled cloves with the fresh chilli, adding a tablespoonful of oil and two of vinegar when they're squished and pastelike.

Using your fingers, rub this paste over the scored skin, pushing bits into the cut lines of rind. Stagger across to the oven and put in the tray, leaving it for 30 minutes. Meanwhile, into the bowl in which you mixed the paste, pour the two remaining tablespoons each of oil and vinegar. When the pork's had its half an hour, remove it from the oven, switching it to 120°C/gas mark ½ as you do so. Now turn the pork over: I find it easiest to lift it by hand wearing ovengloves. It makes them dirty, OK, but there is the washing machine…

Pour the oil and vinegar over the underside (which is now uppermost on the rack) and put the pork back in the low oven, leaving it there for 23 hours. (Actually, you could leave it longer. One of the joys of this is that it cannot overcook.) Anyway, after 23 hours, or 30–40 minutes before you actually want to eat, turn the oven back to the highest it will go, remove the pork and turn it back crackling-side up. Put it back in the oven for 30 minutes, in which time it will get hot and crisp, though you can give it another 10 if you feel it needs it.

Remove, slice off the crackling in a horizontal swipe of the knife and break it into manageable pieces, then start carving or pulling at the the tender meat.

CREAMY POTATO GRATIN

My not entirely orthodox way of turning out this otherwise classic dish of cream-softened potatoes has a lot going for it here. The thing is, you cook the potatoes first in a pan in the stove, which means that, one, you can do it in advance up to the final and quick blast in the oven (always a boon for me); two, you don't therefore need a double oven, because you blitz the potatoes while the pork's having its post-roasting rest; and, three, this is the best way of making sure the potatoes are actually cooked to margin-blurring softness – there is nothing worse than biting into a potato gratin that bites back.

**2kg floury potatoes, such as King
  Edward or Maris Piper**
500ml full-fat milk
500ml double cream

1 whole onion, peeled
2 cloves garlic, minced
1 tablespoon salt
approx. 50g unsalted butter

Preheat the oven to 240°C/gas mark 8.

Peel the potatoes and cut them into slices, neither especially thin nor especially thick (approx. 1cm) and put them into a large saucepan with the milk, cream, onion, minced garlic and salt. Bring to the boil and cook at a robust simmer or gentle boil (however you like to think of it) until verging on tender, but not dissolving into mush. The pan might be hell to clean afterwards, but any excuse for long, lazy soaking rather than brisk pre- or post-prandial scrubbing always appeals to me. And, for what it's worth, I find that when pans are really, dauntingly, stuck with cooked-on gunge, it's more effective to soak them in hot water and detergent (ie, the stuff you put in the washing machine, though I haven't tried, and don't think I would, with tablets) rather than washing-up liquid.

Use some of the butter to grease a large roasting tin (37 x 30cm) and then, after removing the onion, pour the almost sludgy milk and potato mixture into it. Dot with remaining butter and cook in the oven for 15 minutes or until the potato is bubbly and browned on top. Remove, let stand for 10–20 minutes and then serve.

This is not the most labour-saving way of cooking potatoes, to be sure, but one of the most seductive. And it reheats well as an accompaniment to cold roast pork, or indeed anything, in the days that follow.

STIR-BRAISED SAVOY CABBAGE WITH NIGELLA SEEDS

Forgive the culinary egomania, not meant entirely seriously you do understand, but I bought a tin of nigella seeds in Dean and Deluca, the world's most pulse-quickening food shop, when I was in New York once, and I can't just let it sit in the cupboard unused forever. Actually, this spice is no impossible-to-find delicacy: it's a regular in Indian food, and can be found labelled 'kalonji', in a variety of spellings, or sometimes 'black cumin', in far-from-recherché outlets. Don't think twice, though, about substituting ordinary cumin seeds.

1 large Savoy cabbage or two smaller
3 tablespoons vegetable oil
1 tablespoon nigella seeds
500ml vegetable stock

Maldon salt to taste
few drops soy sauce
few drops toasted sesame oil

Halve the cabbage or cabbages, cut out the core and finely shred it.

Warm the oil in a wide but deep saucepan that has a lid, and patiently toss the cabbage in the oil over a low to medium heat until it's evenly but finely glossed and beginning to wilt. Sprinkle in the nigella seeds and turn well so that they are evenly distributed. Pour in the stock, toss the cabbage again, salt well or cautiously depending on how salty the stock is, and clamp on the lid, leaving the cabbage to steam for 4 minutes or so. Remove the lid and taste to see how cooked the cabbage is. I find that 4 minutes more or less does it for me, by which time I give the cabbage another minute, while stirring, with the lid off. Splash with soy and sesame oil, toss again and transfer to a warmed bowl or bowls.

DEAN & DELU
NEW YORK CITY

Nigella

PACKED BY DEAN & DELUCA NY, NY 10012 NET WT

EASY STICKY-TOFFEE PUDDING

This draws on the culinary technology of the surprise pudding – that amazing affair by which, on baking, a layer of sponge is formed, under which evolves a thick and luscious sauce – while playing with the flavours of a traditional sticky-toffee pudding. True, if you're feeding 12 people you'll need to make two, but given how almost provocatively easy it is, that's no big deal. I can see this stretching to 8, maybe even a little bit beyond, but I wouldn't want to ask much more of it, despite the gargantuan feast that precedes it. Better to have too much than give rise to even the slightest tremor of ration-anxiety at the table. Never Knowingly Undercatered, that's me.

for the cake:
100g dark muscovado sugar
175g self-raising flour
125ml full-fat milk
1 egg
1 teaspoon vanilla extract
50g unsalted butter, melted

200g chopped, rolled dates

for the sauce:
200g dark muscovado sugar
approx. 25g unsalted butter in little blobs
500ml boiling water

Preheat the oven to 190°C/gas mark 5 and butter a 1½-litre capacity pudding dish.

Combine the 100g dark muscovado sugar with the flour in a large bowl. Pour the milk into a measuring jug, beat in the egg, vanilla and melted butter and then pour this mixture over the sugar and flour, stirring – just with a wooden spoon – to combine. Fold in the dates then scrape into the prepared pudding dish. Don't worry if it doesn't look very full: it will do by the time it cooks.

Sprinkle over the 200g dark muscovado sugar and dot with the butter. Pour over the boiling water (yes really!) and transfer to the oven. Set the timer for 45 minutes, though you might find the pudding needs 5 or 10 minutes more. The top of the pudding should be springy and spongy when it's cooked; underneath, the butter, dark muscovado sugar and boiling water will have turned into a rich, sticky sauce. Serve with vanilla ice cream, crème fraîche, double or single cream as you wish.

Serves 6–8.

NOTES

CHAPTER TEN

TEMPLEFOOD

I think I'd better start by explaining what Templefood is: it's my term for the soothing, pure, would-be restorative food I make for myself after one binge or late night too far. 'Temple' as in 'my body is a...'

Well, mine's not, but this is what I eat when I want to feel it is. And don't think – as if – I'm counselling deprivation or restraint, but rather the holy glow of self-indulgently virtuous pleasure...

PRAIRIE OYSTER

How much pleasure you could get out of this I'm not sure, but it's a preliminary rather than regular feature of the restoration process. My templefood times tend to start with, indeed are prompted by, a hangover and so I thought it made sense to start this chapter with a hangover cure. Working on Nietzsche's principle that what doesn't kill you makes you stronger, I won't make any apologies for the daunting concoction that follows. The point is, if you can survive this, you can survive anything.

There's no oyster involved, but the name from this drink comes, I suspect, from the slang term used by ranchers for a bull's testicle, which the egg yolk suspended in the alcohol was thought to resemble – and which I'm sure makes you all feel very much better.

1 egg yolk
40ml brandy (approx. 3 tablespoons)
a few drops malt vinegar

couple of dashes tabasco
a few drops Worcestershire sauce
salt and pepper

Put the egg yolk in a marguerita glass. Mix the remaining ingredients and pour over yolk. Gulp down in one.

Serves 1.

SALMON WITH GREENS AND SHITAKE MUSHROOMS

My templefood days do not consist of fey picking: this is gratifyingly substantial. In order to enjoy it you don't have to know that salmon is rich in Omega-3 oils, which are beneficial, indeed essential, to good health, and that shitake mushrooms are believed, by the Japanese at least, to contain cancer-fighting properties, but it all helps in the aim of wallowing in virtuous well-being.

But the most important thing I can tell you is that this is *good*.

2 skinned salmon fillets, preferably organic

1 clove garlic, finely minced or chopped

2 tablespoons vegetable or groundnut oil

125g shitake mushrooms, de-stalked and sliced

400g choi sum, roughly chopped

3 tablespoons soy sauce

1 teaspoon sesame oil

pepper to taste

Grill or fry the salmon fillets – preferably in a good non-stick pan or on the smooth side of a griddle – until just cooked through and remove them to warmed plates while you get on with or finish the vegetables (you can start them off as the salmon cooks).

In a heavy-based pan, fry the garlic in the oil until it is warm but not catching. Add the sliced mushrooms together with the choi sum stalks, stirring everything together for a bare minute or so. Cover the pan and cook for about 5 minutes, remove the lid and add the roughly chopped choi sum leaves, soy sauce and sesame oil, then let it cook for another 2–3 minutes until the leaves have wilted.

Pile the mushrooms and greens on the plates with the salmon and, pleasurably, eat. I sometimes make a little sauce to go with, by mixing Colman's mustard powder into a smooth paste with a little cold water, adding a few drops of soy sauce and (a Microplane grater makes easy work of this) a scant, pulpy purée of fresh ginger.

Serves 2.

GINGERY-HOT DUCK SALAD

I don't buy into this anti-meat drive. Indeed, I am vehemently pro-protein. Nor am I fat-phobic, so I tend to leave the fatty layer of skin on the duck breast before I griddle (or fry) it, but remove it before cooking by all means if you have succumbed to the lure of the lean. And if that's the case, you'll be pleased to learn that not one drop of oil need go into the dressing. However, I often sprinkle a little toasted sesame oil over at the end, which is why I've still listed it in the ingredients. Your call.

The salad itself is a slight reworking of a Cambodian beef salad I often make; here the lime juice in the steeping mixture (which turns into the dressing) is supplemented with orange juice (Asian evocations of duck à l'orange and all that), but in season, around January, use instead of this combination the fragrantly acerbic juice of one Seville orange.

1 duck breast

2 tablespoons fish sauce

juice of ½ lime and juice of ½ orange, or of 1 Seville orange

1 cayenne chilli, finely chopped

1cm ginger, grated

few drops sesame oil (optional)

50g baby spinach, watercress, lambs lettuce or a mixture

Grill or fry the duck breast – fat-side down if not removed – until it's cooked to juicy pinkness.

Let it rest on a board while you mix the fish sauce, lime and orange juice (or just Seville-orange juice), chilli, ginger and optional sesame oil together in a bowl.

Pour any juices that the duck has made into the bowl, and then carve the meat on the diagonal into thin slices. Toss the sliced duck into the bowl and stir everything well. Turn it out onto a serving plate covered with the salad leaves.

Serves 2.

HOT AND SOUR SOUP

I know that for some people nothing feels more restoring than something warm and unchallengingly bland, but when it's succour and sustenance I need, it's spice that I want. This soup, tom yam – the culinary equivalent of Friar's Balsam – clears the tubes and brings fire to the jaded soul. And there's nothing like a bit of searing heat to push away any hungover seediness. It's good for those days when you're thick with cold, too.

It's easy to throw together: the chicken stock I make out of boiling water and bouillon concentrate, and the tom yam paste is sold now at most supermarkets, along with the other ingredients, too.

1½ litres chicken stock

1 heaped tablespoon tom yam paste

4 kaffir lime leaves, finely chopped

1 stick lemongrass, tender inner part only, roughly chopped

juice of 1 lime

4 tablespoons fish sauce

3 small fresh red or green chillies, finely chopped

1 teaspoon sugar

150g straw or button mushrooms, halved or quartered according to size

500g peeled raw prawns, thawed if frozen

5 small spring onions, cut into short lengths and then into strips

small bunch coriander, chopped

Heat the stock and tom yam paste in a decent sized saucepan with the lime leaves, lemongrass, lime juice, fish sauce, chillies and sugar. Bring to the boil, add the mushrooms and simmer for a couple of minutes, then add the prawns and spring onions and cook for a further 2–3 minutes, or until the prawns are cooked but still tender. Sprinkle with a little coriander and put more on the table for people to add themselves as they want.

Serves 4–6.

VIETNAMESE CHICKEN AND MINT SALAD

This is what I make when a temple-mooded girlfriend or two are coming over not so much for dinner as to talk or moan, as one does, during those chapter meetings of the martyred sisterhood. It's very quick as long as you've got a food processor (and not that time-consuming without) and ideal for picking at with an outstretched fork over a drawn-out evening. The dressing needs to steep for half an hour, but you don't need to do anything to it while it's going on.

This recipe is adapted from *The Best of Nicole Routhier* and is, or so she explains, the Vietnamese equivalent of coleslaw, but this doesn't quite sum up its fresh appeal and ability to spruce up a girl's flagging spirits. This is a real reviver.

Since it's easy to buy chicken breast ready-cooked, that's what I generally use, but obviously if you've got a leftover chicken in the fridge I suggest you use that. Likewise, consider using the baby cabbages you see around these days: they are exactly the size you need and easier than hacking away at a big bruiser. All the less familiar ingredients can, as ever, be bought at a supermarket. And by all means leave out the oil in the dressing if including it would make you feel less than virtuous.

This makes a lot, but I find it's very easy to get through – and it stays in the fridge for a day or two to provide instant midnight pickings of a not-too-injurious sort.

1 chilli, preferably a hot Thai one, seeded and minced

1 fat garlic clove, peeled and minced

1 tablespoon sugar

1½ teaspoons rice vinegar

1½ tablespoons lime juice

1½ tablespoons Vietnamese or Thai fish sauce (nuoc nam or nam pla)

1½ tablespoons vegetable oil

half a medium onion, finely sliced

black pepper

200g white cabbage, shredded

1 medium carrot, shredded, julienned or grated

200g cooked chicken breast, shredded or cut into fine strips

fat bunch of mint, about 40g stemmed weight

In a bowl, combine the chilli, garlic, sugar, vinegar, lime juice, fish sauce, oil, onion and black pepper to taste. Put to one side for half an hour. Then in a big plate or bowl, mix the cabbage, carrot, chicken and mint. Pour over the onion-soused, chilli-flecked dressing and toss very well – slowly and patiently – so that everything is combined and covered thinly. Taste to see if you need salt or pepper. Serve on a flat plate with maybe a bit more mint chopped on top.

Serves 2–4.

PEACHES AND BLUEBERRIES

Pudding is hardly a feature of the templefood way but, as a girlfriend said to me once, you need to know there's something to stave off that moment of desolation that threatens to settle when eating's done for the day. Hence this: which is frankly not so much a recipe as a suggestion. The colours themselves induce great good mood and, allegedly, blueberries aid memory, though I forget now where I read this.

Mostly I eat this cold, the peaches sliced, the blueberries tumbled over them and a few drops of orangeflower water sprinkled on top, but you can – and this is excellent for breakfast, or when you desperately need the comfort of something hot – just dollop some Greek yoghurt (0% fat or otherwise) over the roughly assembled fruit, sprinkled the sparsest bit of demerara sugar on top and then cook in a hottish oven for about 20 minutes – until the fruit's softened and the sugar faintly caramelised. It makes sense particularly to go for the hot option with the leftovers of the first, fresh fruit salad.

These amounts should fill an ovenproof dish measuring approximately 30 x 20cm.

6 peaches
3 punnets blueberries

1–2 teaspoons orangeflower water

It's difficult to say how many this would serve: it would do 8 definitely, but if it helps to have a stash of ready-made cut-up fruit to hand, then don't feel you need to cut down on quantities for even two of you.

For those days when a yielding peach is hard to find – and there are many of them – my other standby is a pawpaw halved avocado-style, the seeds removed, a tumble of raspberries tossed into the now-empty cavity and a reviving, flavour-sprucing shot of lime juice squeezed on top.

NOTES

NOTES

INDEX

American pancakes with wafer-bacon
and maple syrup 10–13

anchovies:
bagna cauda 84

apple and blackberry kuchen 23–4

aromatic lamb-shank stew 189–90

Asian-spiced kedgeree 14–15

asparagus:
soft-boiled eggs with asparagus soldiers
157

aubergines:
soft and sharp involtini 105–6

bagna cauda 84

bananas:
Elvis Presley's peanut-butter and
banana sandwich 140

beans:
chicken with chorizo and cannellini
60–1
pasta e fagioli 108–9
South-beach black bean soup 130

beef:
Granny Lawson's lunch dish 162–5
pasta with meatballs 100

biscuits:
rainy-day biscuits 116–18

bitter orange ice cream 70–2

blackberries:
apple and blackberry kuchen 23–4

Bloody Mary 21

blueberries:
peaches and blueberries 234

borlotti beans:
pasta e fagioli 108–9

Bounties with pineapple, deep-fried 143

Boyle, Tish: *Tish Boyle's Diner*

Desserts 47

bread:
ginger-jam bread and butter pudding
166–8

breakfasts:
American pancakes with wafer-bacon
and maple syrup 10–13
apple and blackberry kuchen 23–4
Asian-spiced kedgeree 14–15
Masala omelette 16
orange breakfast muffins 6
Welsh-rarebit muffins 8

bream with anchovies and thyme 180–2

cabbage:
stir-braised Savoy cabbage with nigella
seeds 215

cakes:
chocolate-chestnut refrigerator cake
171
chocolate cloud cake 110
chocolate fudge cake 47–8
chocolate-lime cheesecake 145–6
Easter nest cake *see* chocolate cloud
cake
see also cheesecake; cupcakes

cheese:
double potato and halloumi bake 36–7
halloumi with chilli 88
Liptauer 161
mozzarella in carrozza 57–8
Welsh-rarebit muffins 8

cheesecake:
chocolate-lime cheesecake 145–6

chestnut purée:
chocolate-chestnut refrigerator cake
171